MW01241722

SCARLET
RIBBONS

MEMOIRS OF EVERYDAY MIRACLES

BONNIE SHANNON BELT

Inspiring Voices
A Service of **Guideposts**

ISBN: 978-1-4624-0410-0 (sc)
ISBN: 978-1-4624-0409-4 (e)

Library of Congress Control Number: 2012922263

Inspiring Voices books may be ordered through booksellers or by contacting:

Inspiring Voices
1663 Liberty Drive
Bloomington, IN 47403
www.inspiringvoices.com
1-(866) 697-5313

All scriptures taken from King James Bible

Printed in the United States of America

Inspiring Voices rev. date: 11/21/2012

SCARLET RIBBONS

Memoirs of Everyday Miracles

Bonnie Shannon Belt

For my Family and all my Angels

CONTENTS

INTRODUCTION

I'D LIKE TO SHARE an occasion which turned out to be one of the most memorable times of my life. As Vern Jackson's agent, I arranged a concert for him in Arizona, where I lived. The pastor of the church and the congregation were very excited to have Vern ministering in music. Everyone loved to see a television artist in person.

A vocalist myself, I was called on first to sing the opening song and then introduce Vern. This was the normal procedure whenever the churches were near enough for me to attend. Vern and his wife Sandra generously allowed this since my testimony was due mostly to them. Tonight, I had inadvertently given the wrong tape to the sound man. While the song, "Scarlet Ribbons" held a very special meaning for me, it was not one I would have chosen for this particular concert. Since it was too late for changes, I gave it my best.

When the concert was finished, we all gathered in the foyer near Vern's tape table. As it usually happened, people sought me out to visit, and while in conversation, a lady interrupted, exclaiming, "It's important that I speak with you immediately!"

Wondering what could be so urgent, I excused myself and followed her to a quiet spot to talk. Although I couldn't imagine what she wanted, I sensed she was in earnest. "I have a message for you from God." she stated simply. "While you were singing, the Lord spoke to me about you and revealed the things I was to tell you. You are to write a book about your life and what He has done for you." Amazed, I stared at this woman whom I'd never seen before, thinking, how could she have known I'd planned to write my story for some time now? Earlier this evening, while getting ready to come here, I'd asked God to let me know what to title my book Only He and I could know about that special prayer.

"Your book is to be called "Scarlet Ribbons", she said, and it will be an inspiration to others. If you seek Him in prayer, He will help you and even the cover will be done supernaturally."

And so I give you, Scarlet Ribbons: Memoirs of Everyday Miracles. A collection of stories intertwined with the scarlet ribbons that represent all He has done for me. My prayer is you'll discover as you read them, it only takes faith the size of a mustard seed to move a mountain.

PART 1:
THE JOURNEY

For we walk by faith, not by sight.

2 Cor. 5:7

THE FAITH OF A CHILD

Luke 18:16

*Suffer little children to come unto
me and forbid them not . . .*

THE MARCH WINDS BLEW briskly, and whipped around my bare legs as I hurried along on that cold Sunday morning in Taft, California. I barely felt the chill for there was determination in every step I took. I was on a secret quest and nothing in the world could have stopped me. An impossible mission, according to a conversation between my grandparents I had overheard the night before. They were discussing the fate of my mother, who was in the hospital, and my heart lurched in my throat when I heard their verdict. According to them, the doctors were saying my mother was going to die!

Long after everyone was asleep, I thought about what I had heard and alternately, worried, and prayed, Please, God, help me! I need a miracle. Just before dawn I came up with a plan to save her. Feeling confident that my solution would work, I fell into an exhausted sleep.

My mother had been ill for some time before I came to stay with my grandparents. Only nine years old, I had no idea how serious her condition was. I just knew she needed care, and for me, that was a labor of love. My mother lived to hear me sing. Her favorite song was one recorded by Perry Como entitled *Scarlet Ribbons*, and I'd learned it for her when I was eight years old. Sometimes, in the middle of the night, when she was the

3

sickest, she'd call out to me. Standing at the foot of her bed, in my long nightgown, I'd sing Scarlet Ribbons over and over. The peaceful look in her eyes warmed my heart so much, I never felt the cold linoleum beneath my bare feet. This situation might have continued indefinitely, had it not been for a visit from a relative. Upon seeing my mother, my aunt immediately called an ambulance. Medical tests revealed that Mama was suffering from a disease of the liver.

Now, I could hardly believe she was lying in a hospital bed close to death. Feeling the need to hurry, I picked up my pace and began to pray again. Please, God, let my idea work! I want my mother back! I don't want to live with Mama's parents.

Life with my grandparents was different from what I was used to. Grandmother was very strict and unlike Mama, ruled her household with an iron hand. Some of the chores she assigned to me were washing the dishes and setting the family table. The pretty, yellow, Formica dinette, trimmed with shiny chrome, had to be re-set with clean dishes after every meal.

"Don't forget the extra place setting." My grandmother often reminded me. Puzzled by her request, I finally worked up the nerve to ask why. "I'm hoping one of my children might come home unexpectedly." Years later, the memory of that empty chair at her table inspired me to write the song *Around Mama's Table* which marked a turning point in my life.

The only break, in the otherwise dull routine, was attending my grandmother's church on Sunday morning. She didn't attend, but insisted I go. I always obeyed because frankly, I was a little afraid of the stern woman.

Now, walking rapidly toward my destination, I wondered what my punishment would be if Grandmother discovered that I'd sneaked away from her church this morning. The act (she would label willful) might warrant a spanking, but I didn't care. My mother's life was at stake. The very thought of losing her brought burning tears to my eyes, and the added threat of ending up motherless struck fear in my heart. I had to do something to save her! Before falling asleep last night, I'd remembered hearing a conversation between two ladies in the pew behind me at church last week. They were talking about a famous lady evangelist who was coming to a near-by church this Sunday to hold a healing service. That's where I was going on this beautiful morning: To ask the visiting minister to pray for my mother. In my young mind, I reasoned if the woman worked for God, then surely He would listen to her. The service had already begun as I walked into the little white church and slipped into the nearest seat. The faith-healer, all dressed in white, looked like an angel standing at the altar. Lifting her head to address the congregation, it seemed she was looking straight at me when she asked for prayer requests. Suddenly shy, it took all the courage I could muster to raise my hand. When she smiled and invited me to come forward, I walked down the aisle with renewed hope.

She quoted the passage from the Bible about the faith of a little child, and used me as an example for her sermon that followed. Standing in for my mother at the altar, I was prayed for, blessed, and sprinkled with holy water during that unforgettable service. I walked out of the church a true believer.

Merrily skipping home, I held tight to my firm conviction that Mama was healed. Convinced she was coming for me soon, I packed my bag and hid it under my bed. To everyone's amazement, except mine, my mother came to get me a month later. It was the happiest day of my life! After hugging Mama, and making God a solemn promise to always take care of her, I ran to get my suitcase.

The memory of that wondrous day remains fresh in my mind today. I think of it as the time a miracle took place in a small, desert town in California. Then I give thanks it happened to me, on the day I first believed!

AND THE WINNER IS. . .

And thine ears shall hear a word

behind thee saying, this is the way walk ye in it.

Isaiah 30:21

THE SEA OF FACES in the audience were just a blur from where I stood on stage, blinded by the spotlight. I knew they were there though, from the roar of applause when I hit the last note of the song, *Stand By Your Man.*

I walked back to the table where the man who had brought me here tonight awaited his call to the stage. "Good luck, Ned," I said to my opponent and sincerely meant it. When his beautiful baritone voice rang out over the sound system in the opening line of *Rawhide*, I had a moment of misgiving. This man is going to be hard to beat, I thought.

The last thing I wanted to do this Monday evening was perform in a talent show. So when the car broke down earlier today, I really wasn't too upset. When it took the last of our savings to pay the towing charge back to where we were staying, I should have known my mother would think of some way to get me to the contest that paid big bucks. "You can just call that nice man, Ned, and ask him to take you," she said.

"Not on your life!" I retorted, "I refuse to call my biggest competitor and ask for a ride. I doubt that he'd want to anyway, since I've won the last two shows."

"Competition is the name of the game, my mother replied, and you'll never know if you don't call." " Besides, we need the money to rent an apartment."My ears perked up at that statement. "Did you say, rent an apartment? And settle down for a while?" I asked eagerly.

"Well, that depends on whether you win tonight. Do you think you can?"

"Consider it done!" I answered with confidence, heading to the telephone. Ned Wilson, one of the best amateur male vocalists in the San Jose area, seemed pleased to hear my voice, and there was only the tiniest pause when I told him why I was calling. But, perfect gentleman that he was, he graciously assured me he'd be happy to take me to the talent show that night.

While he drove, I couldn't help but wonder what he was thinking. We had both been doing the talent show circuit for some time now. My mother, a shrewd business woman with an eye and ear for money-making opportunities, had promptly entered me in the first contest that she'd heard about. I wasn't keeping score, but Mama was. According to her, I'd won twenty-one to date and the ones that I'd lost had been to this man driving beside me. I wondered if he might later regret helping a lady in distress.

The club was filled to capacity when we arrived. There was a lot of talent in the area, and the locals all came to root for their favorites. The large turn-outs allowed the clubs to pay the winners well and still make a profit. Many musicians and singers competed for the prize money to supplement their incomes with quick cash. I was an old hand at it by now, but this did nothing for my pre-stage nerves tonight; there was too much at stake. If it meant settling down, I desperately wanted to win. I was tired of life on the road.

After that night, some time ago, when I had been chosen by a country band to be their female vocalist on tour, Mama had made up her mind. If she had anything to do with it, I would become a famous recording artist just like her favorite singer Jody Miller. I'd been hired on the spot when I sang Jody's hit, *Queen of The House* (the only song I knew besides *Scarlet Ribbons* which I'd sung to Mama when I was a child)Over the next few years I perfected my craft, learning dozens of songs to sing on every stage Mama could gain entrance to. She'd march up to the band-leader and using her best sales pitch, "You're in for a treat tonight!" convince him to let me sing.

After the first eight bars the band would give her a nod of approval. Beaming, Mama would give them her best "I told you so!" smile. It was clear to everyone she was my biggest fan. Now, tension mounted as Ned and I sat waiting for the judges to make their choice. I said a little prayer that we'd remain friends, whatever the outcome. Just like I'd suspected, a decision couldn't be reached. The officials called five singers back to the stage. Ned and I exchanged a smile. We were both in the selected group. This time we were to be judged by the applause of the audience. The crowd went wild after Ned sang. To my sheer delight, they also whistled and applauded when I finished. Finally, it was decided we were tied for first place. Ned and I were asked to sing yet again. I was relieved when he was called to perform first; I had some praying to do! Ned was known for songs from the musical, *Oklahoma* and when his powerful voice hit the first notes of the tune, cheers broke out in the audience. Happy for him, yet a little envious of his song, I couldn't help thinking, *It'll take a miracle to win this thing!* While trying to make a song choice, I heard the words, *sing the new one.* I looked around to see who had voiced them, but I was the only one at the table. I'd just learned *I Never Promised You a Rose Garden.* Trouble was, I'd never rehearsed it with a band. Deciding to try it, I gave the song my all. A thundering roll of applause was my reward. Once again we waited to hear those famous four words: And the winner is . . . Thankfully, it was me! Along with the money, I received a gift certificate for a very expensive pair of western boots which I presented to Ned for all his help.

The next night on the way to Reno to sing at the Mapes Hotel (an offer we couldn't refuse) I thought, isn't it strange how things work out when God is in charge. I'd gone to the talent show to win . . . so I could quit . . . yet, here we were on the road again!

Looking back at that night, I can see God's plan for my life. The journey was mapped out. By following Him, the still, small voice would lead me to Arizona where the man of my dreams waited for me.

BONNIE SHANNON

IT HAD TO BE GOD

For this God is our God

for ever and ever

He will be our guide even unto death.

Ps.48:14

WE HAD BEEN IN Phoenix, Arizona for two days and already Mama wanted to go back to California. But, who could blame her? The temperature was a sizzling one hundred-ten degrees outside, and we had no air-conditioning in our car! As a professional singer, I wondered how this hot dry climate would affect my voice. The money I earned from singing had to support three of us now.

After appearing in Reno, Nevada, Mama and I decided to take a break from our quest for a recording career for me. I went back to work in an office, where I met someone I thought I'd spend forever with. But the only blessing to come out of that relationship was my son, Scotty, the apple of his Grandma's eye. A single mother now, Mama and I, along with Scotty, went on the road again, hoping this time for success.

We traveled from Bakersfield to Nashville and back to Los Angeles where after auditioning for a USO show, I did my patriotic duty and entertained the troops.

Thinking we might like Arizona, I'd brought Mama and four year old Scotty here to the Valley of the Sun to visit friends. When they learned we were cutting our visit short, they suggested we all have a night on the town before leaving. My friend Jo Ann, who liked to hear me sing, invited some of their friends to go along. One of them, Leroy, was successful in arranging a guest spot for me everywhere we went. He seemed to know every musician in town.

We ended our night out at the Nite Life Club in West Phoenix. Leroy knew the owner, Dick Belt, and wanted him to hear my vocals. To Leroy's disappointment, Dick wasn't there. The band asked me to sing, and I was thrilled to discover the drummer was the singer who had recorded one of my favorite songs playing on the radio. His name was Ron Lowry, and his song, *Marry Me* was making the charts. Getting his autograph made the whole trip to Arizona worthwhile to me! Deciding to call it a night, we went back to our friend's house to pay the baby-sitter and pack the car for our early morning departure to California. Mama was adamant about leaving. We'd settled down for a few hours sleep when the phone rang. It was Leroy. "Listen, could you stay one more night? I drove back to the Nite Life Club at closing time. I told Dick Belt about you, but he'd already heard! He'd like to hear you sing." Putting the phone down, I went to ask Mama if she wanted to stay. Answering in her usual out-spoken way she said, "No! The sooner we leave, the happier I'll be." Suddenly relenting, she said, "I suppose I can stand one more day, if you want to stay." Both of us were unaware her change of mind would alter the course of our lives. The next night Leroy took us to meet Dick Belt. Apparently impressed with my Patsy Cline songs, the tall, handsome man offered me a job on the spot. As I stood looking into his smiling blue eyes, I had no idea that soon I'd be calling him my Prince Charming. At that moment I just knew I felt comfortable in the nightclub, and I liked this man with the engaging personality. I accepted the job without consulting my mother. Surprisingly, Mama agreed to it. Possibly, because she thought it would be temporary. Singing engagements didn't usually last more than a couple of weeks, and of course we could always use more money to get to the next one, but there wouldn't be another job. Four months later Dick and I were united in Holy Matrimony. Mama went back to California alone. Later, I held the un-official record in Phoenix as the longest performing female vocalist on the same stage nightly. My other claim to fame was when my song *Lovin' You Lightly* became a national break-out on Billboard's Top Country Singles!

Leroy came to the club on our anniversary every year to celebrate with us. He loved to remind us that he, and he alone, was responsible for bringing us together. Privately, I begged to differ with him. When the job lasted twenty years and my marriage to Dick for more than thirty, in my own humble opinion, it had to be God!

BONNIE SHANNON & THE DYNAMICS

FROM THE NITE LIFE
TO A NEW LIFE

Learning to trust Him with each step

I take, I'm walking with Jesus,

the rest of the way . . .

B. Belt

S ATISFIED THAT THE KITCHEN was back in shining order after the
evening meal, I turned off the light, and headed to the next room
to watch television. Having the place all to myself, and a whole hour free
before getting ready for work, I thought I might as well keep my long-
standing promise to Aunt Rose and tune in to her favorite program. The
channel was not one we watched in our household. It was on the Christian
station. We always flipped past it to watch a popular sit-com. The only
thing that stuck in my mind abut this channel was a press release that I'd
seen in the newspaper, about a Christian network, being started here in
Phoenix, Arizona. It was at the same time my opening night as a singer at
The Nite Life was advertised. I remember thinking, while it might benefit
some people, I was just too busy to watch it. True, I'd believed in God since
I was a child, but I hadn't turned to Him in a long. time. Why would I? I
had it all. Married to the man of my dreams, my own Prince Charming,
who'd given me a lovely home, beautiful clothes, and a stage to sing on
for as long as I wanted. Along with the security for me, and my little boy,
I'd been blessed with my husband's loving family. His aunt Rose was my

favorite. She was my biggest fan from the day I stepped on the stage until now. When my song made the Billboard Top100 Country Chart, I was convinced her prayers helped to get it there. The last time we were together, Aunt Rose pleaded with me to tune in to her favorite program.

"Bonnie, you could sing their kind of music. I believe you could even write it."

"Oh, no, Aunt Rose, I protested, I don't know enough about the Bible to write Gospel music. Besides, I don't think it would appeal to the Nite Life crowd." "All I'm asking is that you watch the program one time," she said firmly.

So here I stood, rooted to my spot in front of the television, enjoying some of the best Country music I'd heard in a long time. Listening carefully to the words I realized they weren't typical heartbreak songs, instead the lyrics were all about God. Aunt Rose was right, I thought, I could sing and write this kind of music. After all, God had given me a miracle when I was a child. I knew first-hand the power of prayer.

While watching the program, I felt an over-whelming desire to learn more about Jesus. Bidding the viewers good-night, the host said, "Someone out there wants what we have." Convinced he was talking to me, I dropped to my knees and repeated his invitational prayer to accept Jesus Christ as my Lord and Savior. Bursting with happiness, I felt I'd just made the best decision of my life! I could hardly wait to share this news with Aunt Rose, but it was too late to call her tonight. Instead, I told Audra, our hostess, at the Nite Life Club. "What are you looking so happy about?" She asked, when I came through the door.

"I just invited Jesus into my life!" I announced, pausing for her reaction. "Is He going to come in here?" She asked, her eyes widening slightly.

"I certainly hope so," I said serenely, and went to change into my stage clothes.

In October of that year, my husband Dick and I took Aunt Rose back to Indiana for a family re-union. Settled comfortably in the back of our converted van, I began to write the Gospel songs for my album entitled, *The Rest of The Way.* Aunt Rose sat with her Bible open to confirm the words that seemed to fly out of my head, onto the pages. With every scripture she found to match my lyrics, Aunt Rose exclaimed, "And you said you didn't know how to write Gospel music!"

I found a church to attend and took a waitress from the club with me to be baptized. She didn't come back to work. My own life didn't change immediately, but my family noticed a difference in me. I began to be more aware of others needs than what to wear for my next performance on stage.

Looking back, I can see God equipping me for my new role as a care-giver. The time was fast approaching when my family would need me. He knew I was going to need Him to help me cope with what lay ahead. There was still the promise to fulfill I made Him when I was a child. After He saved my mother, I vowed to always take care of her. Somehow, at nine years old I had the wisdom to know, if I did my part, He would take care of me. Whatever I faced in the future, I knew I'd never be alone. On the day I turned my life over to Him, He made me a promise. It is written in His Word and inscribed on my heart . . . I am with you always.

THE GODSEND

Blessed are the believers

Who believe and yet have not seen

Blessed are they who live by faith

Blessed are those who believe

B. Belt

HIS NICKNAME WAS TACO short for Tuaca. A gentle giant whose looks were so deceiving. One of the largest breeds of dogs, a Great Dane, Taco's size alone would have frightened away any would be attackers. Yet, beneath his huge body, beat the most tender heart of any animal I had ever known.

My son, Scotty, who was five years old, loved him so much that he promptly made him a playmate. Taco seemed to sense that Scotty, an only child, needed a friend, so he tolerated being fussed over by his new little buddy. Taco, a beautiful Harlequin, never batted an eye when Scotty dressed him for the holidays which included, a party hat on New Years Eve, a mask on Halloween, and sunglasses in the summer. As time went by, Taco became so much a part of the family he was like another child to us. When a sore developed on his leg, we were devastated when the report came back . . . Cancer.

Our only thought was keeping Tuaca for a few more years, so with faith I turned to God and began to pray constantly. When my husband Dick and I heard that the University of Arizona in Tucson was experimenting on a cancer cure for dogs, we made an appointment for Tuaca. Treatments were scheduled and we began the weekly one hundred-fifty mile trips. It seemed for a while that he was getting better, but on one particular cloudy day, I felt a sense of foreboding as we started on our trip. In silence I prayed as we drove. Arriving at the hospital, Dick and I sat in the car with Tuaca, not willing to let him him go. Finally, with heavy hearts, we took him in and relinquished him to a nurse. We watched her lead him toward the treatment room and when Taco suddenly stopped and looked back at us with sad, reproachful eyes; it seemed our hearts would break! After the treatment the doctor directed us to his office, seated us, and silently handed me a box of tissues. He didn't have to tell us that we would never see our dog again.

Needless to say, the trip back home was very sad. I dreaded the thought of going back to the empty house, knowing that Tuaca wouldn't be sleeping beside our bed that night. Although we'd tried to prepare Scotty for the worst, telling him that God might need Tuaca more than we did, he still had to be told. Between bursts of tears, I emphatically told my husband, "No more dogs!" About a month later my spirits were lifted by a visit from Dick's Aunt Rose and her husband Harold, whose company we enjoyed. When Rose and I returned from our usual shopping trip, Dick met us at the door with a message from our veterinarian. The doctor called to say he'd found the perfect dog for us.

Still missing Tuaca, I half-heartedly agreed to take the trip across town to look at the dog that was supposed to be perfect. Rose and Harold remained in the car when we arrived at the address, and anxiously waited for us to emerge with a new dog in hand. When a huge Harlequin named Shadrach, bounded into the room and started smothering me with wet, sloppy, kisses, I knew he was going home with us. Rose and Harold were elated when we returned to the car with our new dog.

After we'd been home for several hours and Shadrach had joyfully explored every room in his new home, we remembered his pedigree papers, still in the car. When Dick brought them in and began to look them over,

I noticed a strange look on his face. When I asked him what the matter was, he wordlessly handed me the pedigree.

As I began to read, my faith deepened, and I knew that all my prayers had been heard and answered. Shadrach's pedigree proved it. According to his papers, our new pet's lineage was directly linked with the dog we had lost to cancer. Shadrach was the Grandson of our beloved Tuaca!

THE SHOW MUST GO ON

The thread of life is very slender

It's a very fragile thing

You can't bring back

Those passing hours

'cause they fly away on wings

B. Belt

MY WORDS OF WARNING to my mother, "Wait for me!" were lost in the wind as I stepped out from the back of the car where I was reaching in for supplies. In horror, I saw Mama take a step and vanish into thin air. She had toppled head first over the cliff leading down to the cottage where she lived. It was at least a thirty foot drop. Paralyzed with fear, I was unable to move for a few seconds, my feet seemed planted to the ground. It was like a bad dream I remembered from my childhood, the kind where you try to scream and nothing comes out.

When my senses returned, I ran to the edge of the ravine and forced myself to look down. What I saw made me physically sick. She had landed face down and her neck was at an odd angle. From where I stood she looked like a discarded rag doll. Trembling with fear of the unknown, and dreading what I might discover, I made my way down the steep hill, screaming for help all the way.

"Call an ambulance" I shouted to my brother Keith in the cottage below.

While waiting for help, I thought back over the past week that I'd been here in Santa Cruz, California. A singer by profession, I'd taken time off from the stage in Phoenix to help my mother find a safe place to live. The house she'd resided in for years had been sold unexpectedly, and she was staying, temporarily, in my uncle's guest house. The little white cottage itself was perfect, nestled in a group of trees beside a little creek. It's only fault that there was no easy access to it from the street. Someone before us had tried to cut steps into the side of the hill but the make-shift path was too dangerous for an elderly lady to walk down alone.

Yesterday we had found a new apartment. Just in time for my flight home was scheduled for later this afternoon. Earlier today I had been wishing that I could stay one more day to get them settled in, but certainly not under these conditions! Now, looking at my mother's still body, lying in that curious position, I cried out to the Lord. Why didn't you send angels to save her? But, as it turned out, He had saved her, according to the doctor who treated the minor cuts and scrapes on her face.

"Your mother is a very lucky woman!" He shook his head in amazement. "She could have broken her neck. Take her home and put her to bed. She'll be alright." He said with a reassuring smile. After calling my husband, Dick, in Arizona to let him know why I missed my flight home, Keith and I went back to the cottage to finish packing and cleaning. Though my brother was thirteen years older than me, we'd always had a close relationship. Usually, when I came here from Phoenix we managed a few hours to visit, but this trip there hadn't been time. Now, while we worked we reminisced about old times and the fun we used to have together, especially during my teens.

We talked about things we hadn't thought of in years. Saturday Matinees at the Rio watching the latest Elvis movie. Sunny days at the boardwalk riding the rollercoaster, screaming in Keith's ear all the way down the steep descent, then begging to go again! We laughed, remembering my first pair of high heels that this big brother whom I tagged Ke-Ke had gifted me with. The memory of me, staggering around, learning to walk in them without falling down was funny, but my demonstration all these years later made us laugh even harder! We remembered the trip to Woolworths to buy my first lipstick, Midnight Pink and the Persimmon Sparkle nail polish that didn't match at all. The flowery scented Evening in Paris perfume I drenched myself in, causing Ke-Ke to have a coughing fit, while assuring me I smelled wonderful! When we sat down to take a much needed coffee break, Keith said, "Sis, if anything good could come from Mom's accident, it would be this visit."

Giving him a hug, I agreed, that if it hadn't happened, we would have missed the chance to re-live those cherished times.

Satisfied that my mother was happy in her new apartment, I went home the following day with a feeling of accomplishment. Two weeks later I was summoned back to Santa Cruz by an emergency call. I'd just finished my first show when I got the news. My brother Keith had been struck by a car while crossing the street. He died instantly. In a state of shock, I could hardly comprehend Ke-Ke was gone.

A big fan of my singing, I knew he would have wanted the show to go on. Somehow, I managed to make it through my second appearance. My world in pieces, I stepped onto the stage, wearing a smile I didn't feel, and sang my heart out for my brother. The crowd cheered me on, completely unaware of the loss I suffered. The following week I was back in Santa Cruz singing for Ke-Ke one last time. At his service I sang his favorite song, *You Were Always On My Mind*. During the tribute my thoughts went back to another day two weeks earlier. The last time we were together when we dissolved in gales of laughter at my silly pantomime. The one of me teetering, in my first pair of stilettos. The high-heeled shoes I'd cajoled Ke-Ke into buying me that long-ago Christmas. When I think about the day of Mama's accident, I marvel at the outcome. Especially, when I remember my brother's words: 'If anything good could come from - - - - - -' Neither of us knew it was our last visit . . . only God could know a thing like that.

THE GUITAR

Every good gift and

every perfect gift

is from above . . .

James 1:17

Awriter for the Santa Cruz newspaper might have reported the incident that happened in June of Nineteen Eighty Four as a case of the victim being in the wrong place at the wrong time, but, to me, it was a tragic end to my son's sixteenth birthday.

After trying a dozen times, to persuade my husband to buy our son, Scotty, a guitar for his birthday, Dick's answer had been an emphatic, "No!" "But it would mean so much to him, I pleaded, guitar is his favorite instrument."

"The last time I spent money on a musical instrument for him, Dick argued, he lost interest in it in a matter of weeks and where is it now? gathering dust under his bed!"

"No, I'm not wasting any more money on one of his whims, and that's final." Trying to reason with him, I pointed out that Scotty had only taken up the trumpet because the class in guitar had been full when he'd signed up for band in school. When this failed to change Dick's mind, I decided to let the matter rest.

Scotty was spending the summer with his grandmother in the ocean-side town of Santa Cruz, California. We were planning to drive there from our home in Phoenix, to surprise him on his birthday. While I packed for the trip, I tried to think of an alternate gift, but I knew that nothing else could compare to the guitar that he'd had his heart set on for so long. I didn't believe that something so important to Scott could seem trivial to God, so, after a fervent prayer, I turned it over to Him.

Scotty's birthdays had always been so much fun in the past. I'd always tried to make his parties memorable, each one better than the year before. We had been to the zoo, the circus, a carnival, skating, golfing, boating; you name it, we had done it! But this year, as a grown-up of sixteen, he had his own agenda. He and his best friend Ian were going to a beach party; where the action was, or so they thought.

If only we had known how their plans were going to turn out!

Scott had been spending summers with grandma in the town by the sea for several years now and he loved it. But then, who wouldn't love a little city complete with a boardwalk and a roller-coaster. Right from the start he had made friends. One of them, Ian, was a particular favorite of mine and grandma's. He was a handsome boy with a beautiful set of manners that endeared him to Grandma. Ian always took the time to talk with her and seemed genuinely interested in her welfare. The two boys were always together and one of their favorite haunts was the beach near Grandma's house. They liked to swim, surf, and of course, watch the girls.

Still lost in my thoughts of the boys I realized that we had reached our destination. When we pulled up in the driveway of grandma's house, Scotty ran out with open arms. After we had a short re-union with my mother, Dick told Scotty, "Get in the car son, we're going to buy you some clothes for your birthday." I turned away, not wanting to see the disappointed look on Scott's face. But when we arrived at the mall, Dick surprised Scott when he said, "I suppose you can direct us to the music store?"

Thirty minutes later we all walked out of the guitar shop in a celebratory mood. A smile on his face, Scotty was proudly carrying a shiny, black, Gibson Explorer. He could hardly wait to go home and show his birthday gift to his friend Ian. When Dick and I went to our motel room after dinner, the boys were enjoying the new guitar so much that they hardly noticed when we left.

The next morning the phone rang early and I was surprised to hear Scott's voice when I answered. The stress in his voice was so apparent that I came awake instantly. "What is the matter," I asked.

"It's Ian, Mom, he's dead. He was killed on the beach last night!" Reeling with shock myself, I finally managed to calm Scotty down enough to piece the story together. Enthralled with his new guitar, Scotty had changed his mind about going to the party and Ian had taken a girlfriend instead. No one knows exactly what happened that night. Only that Ian had been stabbed to death by a hostile gang while trying to protect his girlfriend from their advances. "Mom, I've lost my best friend on my birthday! Scotty said, his voice shaking. "It might have been me, if it weren't for my new guitar." "Ian wanted me to go with him, But I wanted to stay home and practice so I told him to go on without me." While putting this experience on paper I almost abandoned telling it because of its bittersweet outcome. However, I happened to hear a report on local television about a man whose son was murdered in the same way, the same place. While the two incidents took place years apart, the circumstances were identical. The man was from Arizona and had taken his children to Santa Cruz, California for a vacation. He had dropped them off at the beach and when he returned to pick them up, he received the news that his son had been killed by a gang who had stabbed him to death while he was defending a young girl. After hearing this, I felt compelled to share what happened to my son. Perhaps this man would read our story someday and know that he is not alone. We share his sorrow.

Today, Scotty is an accomplished, professional guitarist. While every birthday is a painful reminder of the loss of his best friend, he, too, is grateful for the gift he received from God that fateful summer . . . the guitar.

THE WONDER OF YOU

In Heaven they're having a party tonight

The stars in the sky are shining bright

The Lord is smiling with sheer delight

'cause one more soul has seen the light

B. Belt

THE NIGHT AIR WAS crisp and chilly as I leaned over my brother's bed to close the window. "No, Please, Ron protested, "Leave the window open. I want to hear the carolers when they come." Carolers? . . . I suddenly remembered and turned away so he couldn't see the stricken look on my face. Ron was dying and he was only forty-five. "You did call the pastor and remind them to come, didn't you Bon? I'm sure it was tonight," he went on excitedly, pulling himself up in his bed to look out the window again. "They should be here any minute!" My heart aching, I went into the darkened living room, where my mother was taking an after-dinner nap, and dropped into a chair. How could I have forgotten something so important I silently admonished myself. After all, my brother didn't have much to look forward to. Ron had stage four colon cancer. My thoughts went back to the day, two weeks ago, when I picked him up at the hospital in Bakersfield to bring him home. It was his second stay there. The first time was on Thanksgiving Day when they removed his colon, and equipped him with a colostomy bag. After they sent him home, complications set in and he had returned to the hospital. I called him every night from Phoenix to give him support but I knew his prognosis was not good. His doctor advised me to come. It would be Ronnie's last Christmas. I boarded the plane in a heartbroken daze.

Our mother met me at the hospital and because of her age stayed in the background while the nurses patiently instructed me about Ron's medications and the proper way to bandage his wound. As I stood, overwhelmed, trying to take it all in, Ron had piped upwith his old sense of humor, "Surely you're not going to trust my sister to do that? Why, she faints when she cuts her finger!" Embarrassed, I wished I hadn't shared that story with him. Still, it had lightened the mood and for that I was grateful. It was then that a visiting pastor from a church in Taft stopped in to pray with us. Leaving his card with me he'd said, "Give me a call and I'll send the carolers by."

Determined to make this a Christmas to remember, my husband had said to spare no expense. So, as a surprise, I had rented a beautiful Lincoln Town car to chauffeur Ron around while I was here. When the nurse accompanied us out to the big white car at the curb, the sheer delight on Ron's face was all that I'd hoped for---after convincing him I hadn't stolen it!

The ride back to Taft was luxurious, to say the least, and the night nothing short of magical. We stopped for a Big Mac (Ronnie's favorite fast food) and sang Christmas songs together, like we used to when we were kids. But, the crowning part of the ride was when Ron's favorite song came on the car radio: *The Wonder of You*. Ron summed it all up when he said, "What a wonderful night, my favorite food, my favorite song and I'm going home for Christmas!" Suddenly, Ronnie declared from the back seat, "Someday, Bon, I'm going to get you a car like this and that's a promise!" Thankful that he couldn't see the tears in my eyes, I was saved from answering with the appearance of a tall steel, oil derrick, up ahead lighting up the night in brilliant color. The sight of that majestic rig, which had been decorated every Christmas, since we were children, was the perfect end to the ride home. Silently, I thanked the Chevron Oil Company for carrying on the tradition of lighting that oil rig every year. Now, a week later, I sat on the chair praying for a miracle to make this night complete. The stillness in the room was suddenly broken by the faint sound of bells, followed by the unmistakable clip-clop of horse's hooves. My heart leaped with joy when I heard voices lifted in harmony singing *It Came Upon A Midnight Clear*. I rushed to the couch and nudged my sleeping mother. "Wake up Mom, the carolers are here!" I looked out across the front porch to see them on the street side of our fence. Looking like a Christmas card, there they were... sitting on bales of hay in the back of the wagon bundled up in scarves and mittens . . . . their frosted breath sending little puffs of white clouds into the air. What followed was the most beautiful concert I had ever heard, sounding better to my ears than the Mormon Tabernacle Choir, for this was the last Christmas my brother would be alive to hear these wonderful songs. I peeked into Ronnies room to see him gazing out the window, listening intently, a look of child-like rapture on his face. When finally, they ended with *We Wish You a Merry Christmas*, I called out our thanks and drying my eyes, went into Ron's room. As I leaned over his bed to close the window, he reached up to touch my face and said, "Thanks, Bon for making this an old-fashioned Christmas!"

I swallowed and managed a smile. "Don't thank me, thank God." Shortly after the New Year, the angels came for my brother. It was at his funeral that the mystery of the carolers was solved. Our cousin Marie told me that she had happened to see the pastor on the street that day and asked them to come by. I missed Ron terribly and thought of him often, especially when I'd hear his favorite song *The Wonder of You*. But it was some years later that I would most vividly recall this particular Christmas season.

While searching for a good used car in the Phoenix newspaper, an ad caught my eye. Lincoln Town Car – Must Sacrifice – Family Crisis. Instantly, my thoughts went back to that starry night driving Ron home from the hospital. If only for sentimental reasons I felt compelled to call the number in the ad. I was pleasantly surprised when the owner gave me the price, an affordable one, and invited us to come and see the car.

Of course we fell in love with the beautiful Lincoln on sight. Though not the exact one I had rented for Ron, it was the same color and model. After taking it for a test drive, we sat with the owner in the luxurious car and discussed the merits of the sound system, Eventually the conversation turned to music. My husband Dick then mentioned that I was a singer and songwriter. The owner straightened up in the plush leather seat and said proudly, "Well, I happen to have a songwriter in my family, too."

To be polite, Dick inquired if we might know any of the writer's songs. The car owner unknowingly sealed the deal, and fulfilled my brother Ron's promise to me, when he answered, "Among the songs he wrote, the most famous was recorded by The King of Rock and Roll. You might remember, *The Wonder of You.*"

PART 2:
THE PROMISE

Stand still and consider the wondrous works of God.

Job 27:14

THE VOICE OF AN ANGEL

For He shall give His angels

charge over thee, to keep thee in all

thy ways

Ps. 91:11

IT WAS DARK OUTSIDE when I walked out of the convalescent home in Bakersfield, California where I had spent the day with my mother getting her settled in for a four week stay to recuperate from hip surgery. I had mixed emotions about leaving her. Part of me felt like I was abandoning her, another part relieved she was in good hands.

Not to worry, I consoled myself, she'll be alright. After all, I'd left her my cell phone in case she got lonely and wanted to call me at my friend Janice's house in near-by Taft, where I was staying. Glancing at my watch as I got into my rental car, I could see that I was going to be late for dinner with my friend. Since Taft was forty miles away and Mom had my cell, I'd have to find a pay phone and call Janice.

California Avenue is a busy street lined with restaurants, gas stations, hotels, and a shopping mall. By heading west on it you can eventually reach the highway to Taft, where I was going now. Surely there would be someplace ahead where I could call my friend and tell her I would be late.

As I drove, my thoughts turned to my husband, Dick who was back home in Phoenix. He'd been here with me three weeks ago when Mom had broken her hip. We'd stayed at a motel on this very street to be near the hospital where she'd had surgery.

My mind on my husband, I almost missed the little convenience store on my right. Pulling in to park, I got out and hurried over to one of the three phones on the front wall of the store. For some reason, what should have been a simple call turned into a major dilemma. No matter how many times I dialed, I couldn't make the connection.

Life just isn't fair sometimes, I thought, staring at the phone in frustration. What I didn't know was that this aggravating experience was going to save me, for someone was watching every move I made! Starting over, I punched in my friends number followed by the digits on my phone card and this time the line was busy. Exasperated, I hung up and started toward my car thinking I could probably drive to Taft, by the time this call went through. Reaching for the car door handle I was suddenly assailed by an indescribable power.

A force that later I could only explain as invisible hands on my shoulders that spun me around in the direction of the phones. When the whirlwind subsided, a loud distinct voice spoke in my ear saying: *Place your call again!* Astonished at the command out of nowhere, I had to comply. I really didn't have a choice. Propelled by energy much stronger than my own, it felt like my body was being guided by a gust of wind. Looking to my left, alarms went off as I locked eyes with a man wearing a plaid shirt, sitting on the hood of his truck. He faced the phone where I had just been and instinctively I knew he had seen me making the first call.

Warning bells, like those clanging at a rail-road crossing, sounded in my head, accompanied by that earlier distinct voice calling out three times in quick succession, *Danger beware! Danger beware! Danger beware!*

My senses fully alerted now, I went to the phone and placed the call again as I'd been instructed. I wasn't surprised when this time it went through. Janice answered the first ring and I told her if I wasn't there soon to call the police. She laughed, thinking I was joking. I didn't have time to explain.

Suddenly the man in the plaid shirt was on the phone next to mine. He was standing so close, I could smell the alcohol wafting from him. Fright stood the hair up on my neck. In a matter of seconds, I was in my car turning onto California Street. My worst driving habit was not checking my rear-view mirror often enough. Probably because I was inclined to daydream. That would not be the case tonight. Looking into the mirror now made my heart race! The blue Chevy truck was behind me! I changed lanes. He did too! The freeway overpass was coming up. Please, Lord, let him turn off! He didn't.

If only I could find the Police Department, I thought, but it was probably behind me, downtown. I couldn't keep going straight or I'd end up on the Taft highway at this man's mercy. Stark terror coursing through my veins, I called out to God: Lord, please, make a way of escape!

Almost instantly the answer came. On the other side of the overpass, rising into the sky like a beacon of hope shining brightly, lighting up the night in welcome was the sign of a motel. The same one where I'd stayed recently with my husband for a week. The night manager would remember me; I would be safe!

The Chevy stayed close behind me, headlights glowing ominously, as I made the necessary two left turns to get into the motel. Familiar with the lay-out of the buildings, I whipped around them, parked in front of the lobby and jumped out of the car. Looking over my shoulder, the blue Chevy was nowhere in sight. I ran into the motel.

Scott, the night manager, recognized me on sight. But his warm greeting quickly turned to surprise when, reaching over the desk, I gripped his wrists and cried,

"Please help me, I'm so scared, there's a man following me!"

"Was he wearing a plaid shirt?" Scott asked, looking over my shoulder.

"Yes!" I answered shakily, tightening my grip on his wrists. "Why?"

"Well, he's walking across the lobby right now. No, don't turn around, he's looking at you and he's not alone. There are two big guys and they're acting weird. I think they're high on something. I'll get security on them right away!"

Scott took me into his private office where I called Janice to give her an update on my whereabouts. This time, when I told her to call the police if I didn't show up, she didn't laugh. I still hadn't calmed down when Scott came back saying, "It's all clear now, the security guards have gone over the entire grounds. Those crazies have fled!"

Thanking him profusely, I went out to the front entrance to my car. My hands still trembling, I turned the key in the ignition and shifted into drive. I'd only moved a few feet forward when I saw it.

Sitting, headlights out, under a street light was the blue Chevy truck. I knew the motor was running; I could see exhaust curling out in little puffs of white smoke. I could also make out the silhouettes of the two men sitting in the truck. Determined, it seemed, to get me!

Slamming on my brakes, I jerked the gear shift into reverse and hit the gas! Almost crashing into the lobby door, I jumped out of the car and ran back inside. Within minutes police cars were swarming the lot. But after all the efforts to catch them, the bad guys had gotten away. It took a while for me to realize that I, too, had escaped. Scott, sensing I was still frightened, sent one of the guards to escort me to the Taft turn-off. When the driver of the security truck flashed his lights and made a U-turn, I found myself alone on the deserted two lane road. There wasn't another car in sight.

Nervous tears rolling down my face, I thought, This is the way it would have been, if not for the extraordinary event that had taken place tonight. If I hadn't heard those strange words of warning, I would have been oblivious to the fact I was being followed. Tailed by pursuers whose truck could have easily over-taken my little rental car and ran it off the road. Tonight had been a wake-up call for me, I thought as I drove. From now on, I promised myself, I'd stop letting my thoughts distract me and pay more attention to my surroundings. After all, who would take care of Mama, if something happened to me? Since my two brothers died, I was all she had.

Strangely, though I kept checking the rear-view mirror, mine was the only car going west on the highway for the rest of my thirty-six mile drive to safety. When I reached the Taft City Limits sign, I breathed a sigh of freedom! Thankful that God, who sees every sparrow that falls, had seen me walking into danger and sent His angel to warn me. Janice was waiting outside when I pulled the car into her driveway. With an anxious look, she asked, "What happened to you tonight? You're white as a sheet!" Knowing I could share anything with Jan, who had been my friend since childhood, I answered her truthfully. "Jan, it was amazing! Tonight, I heard the voice of an angel"

BANDSTANDS TO BEDPANS

He's still the same savior

for all who believe

It's still the same cross

that set us all free.

B. Belt

POISED ON THE EDGE of my seat, I was the first one off the bus when it arrived in Bakersfield, California. Staggering slightly under the weight of a bag on each shoulder, I hurried to find a taxi. "Airport, please," I instructed the driver after climbing into the back seat of his cab. Since being awakened by the insistent ringing of the phone early this morning at my home in Phoenix, Arizona, I'd been a bundle of nerves. The caller, my mother's doctor, after informing me that Mama was in a hospital in Taft, had shocked me completely awake when he added, "Get here quickly, she has three days to live at the most." The fastest way to get there was a flight to L.A., then a bus to Bakersfield, and finally, a rental car to Taft. I knew the route well; I'd traveled it so many times over the last five years to care for my mother. Now, less than an hour away from my final destination, I allowed myself to relax.

Turning my attention to the taxi driver who was talking to me, I noticed a cross hanging from the mirror. Just the sight of it brought me comfort and for the first time that day, I felt hope stirring in my heart. A miracle was just what I needed. "Where did the lovely cross come from?"

I asked the driver. "My boss owns more than twenty taxicabs with a cross in every one. He's a Catholic, and me, well, I'm a Protestant, but, in my opinion, it's still the same cross."

"Thank you," I said to him, "I'm a songwriter and you've just given me a new song!"

"Are you really going to write it?" "Yes, I am," I said, smiling at his enthusiasm. I'm going to call it, *The Same Savior.*"

True to my word, I began to write the song as soon as I got into my rental car. Halfway to Taft, I had the lyrics finished, and a simple melody in my head when I arrived at the hospital. Putting my small notebook back in my purse, I was glad I'd remembered to bring it. I also used it to write, what I called, *Little Letters to God* whenever I had a problem I couldn't handle by myself. Knowing I'd need a prayer partner I'd written to Him on the flight to Los Angeles this morning, asking Him to send someone. The nurse was attending my mother when I walked into the room. Looking up, she gave me a welcoming smile. Introducing myself, I asked her about Mama's condition. "We need to pray!" she said. "The doctor doesn't think she'll make it." He had sent me a nurse after my own heart. One who walked in faith, as I did, and believed in the power of prayer. Together, we asked God to heal my mother and grant an extension on her life. Grateful for the support of this lovely Florence Nightingale, I shared with her the song I'd written that morning. Her response came as a surprise when she said, "Come on, let's go make someone's day!" I followed her to the emergency room, where she insisted that I sing *The Same Savior* to the crew. Rewarded with a rousing, round of applause, I was thankful there weren't any patients being treated at the time.

Back in my mothers room, I sat by her bed praying that she would wake up. But her doctor was less than encouraging when he came in to examine her. Explaining her condition to me (a vascular disease) in medical terms that I couldn't understand, he offered me no hope at all. Instead, he had some advice: "Put her in a nursing home and go on with your life." Adding, "If she wakes up," he went to his next patient. The nurse, who I now considered a friend, implored me to take a break.

"Get some rest, she said, I promise I'll call you if she flickers an eyelash."

"I'll go, I finally agreed, but don't give her chocolate ice cream when she wakes up."

"Why not," my new friend asked, with the hint of a smile at my positive attitude.

"Because, I answered, smiling back at her, she doesn't like it."

Instead of going to mama's empty house to wait by the phone, I decided to drive around the small town of Taft, where I'd spent my childhood. Passing familiar landmarks, I was surprised at the buildings still standing. Even the church, where I had prayed for my mother so long ago, looked the same. I had gone there with the faith of a child expecting a miracle, and the experience changed my life. My mother recovered, and in return I promised God to always take care of her. I'd finally come full circle.

If He saved her this time, I was ready to make any sacrifice to keep her from spending the rest of her life in a nursing home. Keeping my promise would include the life changing decision to leave my home in Arizona. My heart ached to think of leaving everything I held dear there, especially my husband Dick. But I wouldn't be alone. Staying true to one of my songs I was: *Walking with Jesus the Rest of the Way.*

My mind made up, I drove back to the house to wait for the news. The phone was ringing while I dug in my purse to find the door key. The caller was Mama's nurse. "Your mother is wide awake and asking for you!" She announced triumphantly.
"And guess what, she went on in the same tone, you were wrong about one thing."

"And what might that be?" I asked, tears of joy filling my eyes. "She does so like chocolate ice cream, she just ate a whole bowl of it."

Several years later, while speaking at a church in the Taft area, I shared this story after singing my song, *The Same Savior.* The audience laughed when I got to the part about the chocolate ice cream. But their laughter turned to sympathy when I relayed my regret I could never find the nurse again, to thank her. I told them of the special trip I'd made back to the hospital, my disappointment at not finding her there, and how I wished my prayer partner could see my mama now! Suddenly, there was a rustle in the crowd as someone stood to their feet. All eyes turned to the woman standing in their midst, and a hush fell, even before she began to speak. Smiling in Mama's direction, the surprise guest turned to me and announced, "I am the nurse who prayed with you that day." Overjoyed to see her, I didn't question how she came to be there. In my heart, I just put it down as another one of His Divine Appointments. Applause broke out when I reached, with open arms, to greet my long-lost friend.

MY BUTTON ANGEL

Be not forgetful to entertain strangers

for thereby some have entertained

angels unawares

Heb. 13:22

LORD, PLEASE SEND SOMEONE to accompany me, I prayed when I stepped out of my car and surveyed the packed parking lot. Checking my watch, I knew the service had begun. In the beautiful church foyer, not a single soul was in evidence. Peeking through the window on the sanctuary door, I could see the pastor was already delivering his sermon.

Too shy to walk in by myself, I stepped back to leave. Turning, I almost knocked down the woman who'd walked quietly up behind me. Coming face to face with the pretty lady, she dismissed my shocked apology and asked a question which took me, even more, by surprise. "Would you mind to button me up? I can never seem to reach that middle button on the back of my dress."

Returning her smile, I agreed on one condition. That she'd walk into church with me! After the service, I explained to her I was new to the area and looking for the right church to attend. I went on to tell her, while this one was similar to my own in Phoenix, I thought the drive was too far, and I might be late every week! We visited a while longer and exchanged telephone numbers, promising to keep in touch.

My new friend kept her word and called me the following week.

"I've been praying for you, and God told me the church you need to attend. I'll take you there and introduce you. You are going to love this pastor, he's a former country singer, just like you."

My button angel was right. Vernon Carr became my pastor and his lovely wife Joyce, my friend. I was blessed to attend their church the entire time I was in Bakersfield. Yes, God sent an angel to show me the way. He knew I'd recognize her since we were a lot alike. Besides the love we each had for the Lord, there was something else we had in common. I couldn't fasten the middle button on the back of my dress either!

FORTY TWO DOLLARS
OF FAITH

For I Know now, whatsoever thou

wilt ask of God

God will give it to thee

John 11:22

THE EARLY MORNING SUN felt warm on my back as I lifted Mama's wheel chair into the trunk of the car. Glancing at my watch, I was happy to see that we were going to be right on time. We liked to be there every Wednesday morning when the doors opened. Other people might look forward to Friday, but not us. We could hardly wait until the middle of the week. On Wednesday, we had places to go and things to see. Well, actually, we only had one place to go, but we could spend hours there, exploring every nook and cranny. Our destination, in downtown Bakersfield, was easily the largest thrift store around. Three stories high, it held a myriad of treasures, and every Wednesday was Sale Day!

After backing the car out of the driveway, I reached up to adjust the rear view mirror and caught a glimpse of my eyes. I was surprised to see new wrinkles around them that I hadn't noticed before. Caring for my mother didn't allow much time for maintaining my complexion. I was completely out of the expensive face cream that I had used back home in Phoenix, and there was no room in the present budget for luxuries like that. Still, my appearance was important because I had future plans for a music ministry.

Before coming here to care for my mother a year ago, I had been a professional singer and had written a gospel album that I wanted to share with others. Driving toward town, I decided to turn my lack of skin cream over to God. He was the One who supplied all my needs I knew I could ask Him for anything.

Toward the end of my prayer, Mama interrupted, "Who are you talking to?" Mama was deaf, but I knew she understood when I pointed upwards, for she said, "As long as you've got Him on the line, will you ask for something we both need?" Smiling at her casual approach, I hoped God had a sense of humor regarding colorfulcharacters like my mother. She went on, "Ask Him for a handicapped space in front of the thrift store, then you won't have to push me so far." She smiled, as though she had just solved the problems of the world. Finishing my own prayer, I assured Him that I didn't need the fancy skin cream that cost forty two dollars, I'd be happy with any kind. Then, I thanked Him in advance for answering both prayers, although personally, I thought it was a lot to ask for. When we arrived at the thrift store, there were no parking spaces, of course, and I had to park the car a block away. Still, nothing could dampen our spirits. Wednesday was here at last and we were going shopping! We had a great day and went home, already looking forward to next week. When the next Wednesday finally rolled around, we decided to get an earlier start to make a doughnut stop. Mama adored maple bars so I always put a little extra cash aside for the bakery, along with our weekly shopping spree money. Business was booming as usual when we arrived at the thrift store, and I knew from experience that finding a parking spot would be difficult. But I'd gladly push Mama's wheelchair a mile to get us to the store where we had such fun together.

Mama almost spilled the last of her coffee when I suddenly braked the car, and put it into reverse. I could hardly believe my eyes! And to think, I had almost missed it. But yes, there it was, right in front of the store. An empty space with a very official sign that read: Handicapped Parking Only. My mother, who was legally blind, peered through the windshield in awed silence. Finally, finding her voice, she asked, "Is that what I think it is?" "Yes, Mama, it looks like your prayer has been answered." What a wonderful way to start the day, I thought, as I wheeled Mama into the store and headed to the elevator. The elevator itself was a blessing. Without it, we would be stuck downstairs all day. Mama's favorite floor was at the top where all the dishes were displayed She was somewhat of an authority on them having made her living for years as an antique store owner. She insisted on examining each dish and because she was unable to see well, it could take a while! While waiting in line at the check-out stand, something on the jewelry counter in thecorner of the store, caught my eye. In all the times we'd shopped here, I'd never seen any cosmetics. But, since this was a day for miracles, I went to inspect the white box. I immediately recognized the name written in gold as the same expensive skin cream I used to buy. Holding the elegant box in my hand, I could almost feel the silky cream on my face and smell its clean, fresh scent. The shrink-wrap was still intact. Whoever donated this luxurious cream hadn't even bothered to open it, much less try it!

Some people won't believe this, I thought, they'll say it was just a coincidence. But, when I turned the box over I knew it was not. On the bottom, the price that the previous owner had paid was clearly stamped: Forty Two Dollars. The store price was five dollars and ninety nine cents. And the best part? It was Sale Day and everything in the store was half off. In His perfect timing, God not only supplied my skin cream, He got me a bargain. The total cost at the register was only three dollars! Long after the jar was empty, I kept it as a precious reminder that nothing is too small, or too big for God. He knows exactly what you need, even before you ask. What else amazed me, was the entire time we lived in Bakersfield, the handicapped space was always empty on Wednesdays. It seemed to be reserved just for us!

OPERATION FAITH

Jeremiah 29:11

For I know the thoughts that I think

toward you, to give you a future and a hope

THE PUNGENT SMELL OF burning bacon brought me to my senses where I stood in front of the television set, mesmerized by the voice of Vern Jackson. The singer was a popular new addition to the program I watched every morning. A professional singer myself, I appreciated his talent and loved his new song, *Higher Than I've Ever Been*. His beautiful voice kept me company every morning while I cooked Mama's breakfast. An invalid, my mother depended on me for everything. Oh no, I've done it again! I thought, as I ran to the stove to retrieve the smoking skillet from the burner. I'd turned it too high as usual. Mama liked her bacon crisp, not half-burnt like I'd been cooking it since Vern Jackson came on the scene.

After eating, she'd usually go back to sleep and I'd have a precious hour to myself. While washing the breakfast dishes I would begin my daily conversation with God. This morning I could hardly wait to get started for I had a special prayer request concerning a box on the top shelf of my closet.

Two years ago, I'd given up the the stage in Phoenix, Arizona where I'd sung nightly for seventeen years. Turning my life over to God, I'd written and recorded an album of Christian songs. My dream was to start a Gospel music ministry.

Shortly after that, the urgent call had come from my mother's doctor in Bakersfield. "Come at once." he said, "I don't expect your mother to live more than three days."

Panicked, I rushed to her side. Miraculously, my prayers were answered and she recovered. Still, she needed constant care and I was faced with the hardest choice I ever had to make. In the end, I couldn't bring myself to put her in a nursing home, so with the support of my husband, Dick, I decided to stay in California and take care of her myself.

This morning while the birds chirped in the tree outside, and the sun streamed in the kitchen window, I began my prayer:

Lord, you know I want to work for you! There are a hundred cassettes in my closet that contain the songs I wrote for your Glory. Please, won't You show me how to do it? I'll take my mother with me in her wheelchair. Please, God, make a way! Immediately the answer came: *Call Vern Jackson.*

I looked around for the speaker but there was no one in the room with me. While I contemplated the command, right off the bat, I could think of at least one reason why I shouldn't call. Vern wouldn't be at the studio. The show that came on in the morning was a re-run of the previous night.. The live shows were recorded in the evening. While thinking this, I heard the words again: *Call Vern Jackson*! Doubting he'd be there, I went to the telephone and dialed the number I'd seen so many times on the bottom of the television screen. You can imagine my surprise when I asked for Vern and a sweet-voiced lady replied. "One moment please." But when the next voice came on, "This is Vern, how can I help you?" I was suddenly speechless. When he started to repeat the greeting, I quickly interjected, stumbling over my words. "Mr. Jackson, p-p-please don't think I'm crazy, but, God told me to call you."

"Well, give me a hint Darlin', what do you do?" he asked in a cheerful voice.

"Uh, I'm an old night-club singer, well, not that old, but not young and I take care of my invalid mother and I'm a songwriter."

"Wait a minute, did you say songwriter?" he asked, when I paused to take a breath.

"Yes, yes." I repeated eagerly, "I wrote a Gospel album."

"Perfect!" he said, "I just happen to need one more song for a project I'll be recording called *Hello Mama*. "Think you could write a song for it?"

Could I write it? Of course I could! I thought, as I quickly answered, "Oh, Mr. Jackson, I can write it in three days! I'll even hand deliver it." "Well, you may have to." he said, chuckling, "Since I'll need it by next Friday."

In a daze I hung up the phone uncertain whether to turn a cartwheel or give in to a sudden feeling of panic over: What had I promised to do in three days?

I went to see if Mama was awake instead. I always shared everything with her and I knew she'd be as thrilled as I was. Since she was totally deaf now, our only way to communicate was using a dry- erase board. Grabbing it quickly I wrote: Good News! and handed it to her with a big smile. Since she was also legally blind, I knew from experience, it would take her some time to decipher what I'd written. Dancing back into the living room, whirling in circles, I plopped in a chair to savor the feeling of exhilaration. Suddenly a picture of my grandmother's table with the empty place setting came to my mind and I knew I had the title. But, it would have to wait, Mama was calling and it would take a while to tell her the good news.

The next morning, while cooking breakfast, my eyes fell on my favorite refrigerator magnet. It read: Faith is the substance of things hoped for, the evidence of things not seen. To me, this scripture from Hebrews 11:1 meant to call things that are not as if they were, and then believe with all your heart you already had them. Sounds simple, doesn't it? But it's harder to do than you think. However, that's the way I planned to handle this project. So the minute Mama's eyes closed for her morning nap I was on the phone beginning what I called: Operation Faith.

First, I called a recording studio to make an appointment for the next morning. When I asked for an eleven o'clock the response was, "Sorry, we have no openings." "I'm sure you will have." I answered, undaunted. "I'll be waiting for your call."

"I wouldn't count on it, Miss, we're extremely busy." The man said and hung up.

Next, knowing Mama would need a sitter while I was busy recording my song, we made the eighty-mile round trip to pick up my cousin Carolyn. I already had it planned to drop her off in Taft, where she lived, on my way to deliver the song to Vern. I'd already had the car serviced; it was ready to go. Now, all I had to do was pack, and . . . oh. . . . write the song. "When do we leave?" Mama asked, watching me take out the suitcase. Tomorrow! I wrote on the dry-erase. That night after she was asleep, I went into the living room armed with pen, paper and tape recorder prepared to write the song. The minutes ticked by as I sat waiting for inspiration to come. It came in a mental picture of my Grandmother's extra place setting, in hopes her child would come home. I thought of all the mother's praying for the safe return of their sons and daughters who'd gone to war, off to college or simply went away of their own volition. A mother myself, I could imagine the joy their homecoming would bring. The song seemed to take on wings and write itself. By mid-night, *Around Mama's Table* was born. Destined, I hoped, for success. When the phone rang at nine the next morning, I had a feeling it was the recording studio. I wasn't surprised when the man said, "Our eleven o'clock just opened up!"

Three hours later, Mama and I were cruising down the freeway to deliver the song to Vern, hoping it would bring us a better life. A week after we returned home, I jumped for joy when Vern called to say, "It's a done deal! *Around Mama's Table* is on my new album." Reflecting back on all the blessings the song has brought me, I shiver to think how close I came, to ignoring the still, small voice guiding me. When I asked Vern how he happened to be in the studio when I called, he replied, "Well, I wouldn't have been there normally, but my help was needed in the music department that day."

So you see, while I had my doubts, God's timing is always perfect. He knew exactly where Vern Jackson was, on that beautiful morning. And because I stepped out in faith that day, God not only answered my prayer, He gave me a new song to sing!

ANGEL AT MELODYLAND

Behold, I send an Angel before thee,

to keep thee in thy way

Exodus 23:20

I COULD HARDLY BELIEVE MY eyes when I looked over and saw her walking out of the back parking lot at Melodyland. Blinking my eyes, I looked again. Was she real or just a figment of my imagination? While driving here tonight, I had prayed for an angel to meet us when my mother and I arrived because I knew I would need help. We were late; there were no parking spaces left up front, and it was raining hard now!

Oh Lord, please let her be my angel! I prayed as she walked toward me. "Will you help me?" I blurted out as she came closer. "Of course I will dear" she said, a smile lighting up her pretty face. "Tell me, what I can do for you. Curiously, the rain had stopped. "I need you to stay with her while I park the car." I said, pointing at my mother sitting in her wheelchair. Without waiting for an answer, I got into my car and parked it in the back lot. Jumping over mud puddles in my high heels, I ran as fast as I could to get back to my mother. I'd forgotten to tell the nice lady that Mom was deaf and blind in case she tried to talk to her. When I breathlessly began to thank her, she stopped me.

"You don't know me, but I am here tonight by divine appointment."

"Oh, I know who you are, you're the angel I prayed for!"

Nodding, she went on, "I wasn't coming here tonight because I don't like being late, but my son insisted that my presence was needed here this evening. Now, I know why. Before you called out to me, the Lord spoke to my heart and said, 'There is one of my saints, go and help her.' I want to share something that He showed me about you while you were gone. As I said before, I don't know you, but He does, and He gave me a message for you."

A message from God . . . for me? I thought incredulously, "Are you sure it's for me?"

I started to ask her, but she just smiled at me and continued:

"God said to tell you that he has watched you care for your mother. He has seen every bedpan you've carried, every tear you've shed, and He has heard your cries out to Him. None of your sacrifices have gone un-noticed and He is going to give you every desire of your heart in return for your faithfulness!" So engrossed in this lady's strange message, I hadn't even noticed that a light rain had begun to fall again. As I turned mom's wheelchair toward the entrance of the building, I marveled to myself: An hour ago I'd been driving around looking for this place, and now, here I was with a perfect stranger, listening to a message from God! Later, I would learn that she hadn't even gotten to the best part yet.

Melodyland was not on our itinerary when Mama and I had set out from Bakersfield this morning. I'd been listening to the car radio when I heard an advertisement for an event that was taking place there tonight. Naturally, my ears would perk up at the mention of a healing service by a world famous evangelist. My mother was an invalid and she needed all the prayer she could get. I decided right then: we were going. But the real reason we were in the Los Angeles area was to make a special delivery. I had written a song for Vern Jackson last week and wanting to make sure that he got it in time for his recording session, I was hand delivering it to him. I wasn't even sure that he would put it on his album. He hadn't heard it yet. I was simply hoping Vern would like the song. It would change our circumstances if he did! Now, as we continued our way to the entrance, questions were already forming in my mind. Who was she? How did she know so much about me? *Had God really sent her?*

As if she had read my thoughts, the sweet-faced lady turned to me, saying earnestly, "I hope you don't mind my giving you these words of knowledge." "God has blessed me with this gift and I must share it." Perhaps she sensed that I still had some reservations (which I did) for she took my hand and continued with conviction, asking me a question which instantly dispelled all my doubts. The question was one I knew the answer to. Leaning in closer to me, she asked, "Would you happen to know the Gospel singer Vern Jackson?"

Speechless, I nodded. Reaching in my purse, I took out the tape with my song on it and handed it to her. "Vern is the reason that we're here from Bakersfield, he might record my song." I said. We had reached the door to the sanctuary when she pulled me away and spoke again.

"He is going to put your song on his album," she said, handing my tape back. "You're going to work for his ministry at least seven years and you will be blessed!" she added, opening the door for me so I could wheel Mama inside.

When we came out of the inspiring service, still accompanied by our new friend, we had yet another conversation in which she told me about prophesying to Vern a year earlier. I confirmed it the next day with the Jackson's. They recalled the occasion when the lady had told Vern that he would be on national television very soon. Three weeks later, his beautiful voice was blessing thousands around the world. Yes, Vern recorded my song, *Around Mama's Table* which not only helped us financially, it opened the door for me to work for his ministry for more than seven years. And to this day, every time a desire of my heart is granted, I remember a certain angel. The one who answered the call for help, on a rainy night at Melodyland, and delivered a message from God . . . . to press on . . . . for He is watching over you!

THE BIRTHDAY GIFT

Looking unto Jesus

The author and finisher

Of our faith

Heb.12:2

I COULDN'T STOP LOOKING AT my birthday present. I walked around and viewed it from every angle. It was breathtakingly beautiful from wherever I stood. It's been said that beauty is in the eye of the beholder, and to me, it was a magnificent sight to behold. A gift from my husband, Dick, and I would cherish it forever!

The artist, a dear friend of mine, felt that she had been commissioned to paint it after a brush with death left her with an unforgettable image of Jesus Christ. Ten years later while starting an undefined portrait before a local dignitary, she had completed the majestic work of art in an incredible one hundred and thirty five minutes.

Drawn back to it now, by its magnetic appeal, I stood staring into the face of Jesus, Bette Myer's portrait entitled, *The Masterpiece*. His beautiful blue eyes holding me captive, I suddenly wanted to share my birthday gift with the whole world! I'd hung the painting in its place of honor by the front entrance. I wanted everyone who came through the door to see it. People always marveled how alive He looked. Life could be lonely with only my invalid mother for company and the portrait brought me comfort.

I felt such a strong connection to it that often the idea would come to me that I was supposed to do something about promoting it. But, what could I do? I'd wonder to myself, I'm just an ordinary woman, a caregiver at that, and Mama takes up most of my time. I decided to pray about it any way.

A year passed by, and still, I didn't have the answer. Nevertheless, I kept on praying faithfully. Finally, thinking that I should do something, I decided to take matters into my own hands. Remembering an evangelist who had visited my church, I went to the post office to send him a wallet size picture of *The Masterpiece*. Perhaps he could help me. Before mailing it, I asked God to send it back to me if this was not of Him. Although I had confirmed the address, two weeks later, the picture mysteriously came back to me, the envelope stamped: Addressee Unknown. While contemplating this turn of events, a voice from the television set broke into my thoughts.

Turning back to the program I'd been watching, the hostess was saying to her guest. "Did you know that ancient writings say Jesus has blue eyes?" Her words resounding in my mind, I felt sure I'd found the answer to who God wanted to promote it. While I believed He had chosen the right person, I just wondered how He expected me to deliver it to her! He began by changing my life when he answered my prayer for a music ministry I had asked for a chance to sing the Country Gospel songs I'd written after re-dedicating my life to Him. While it didn't seem possible since I was a full-time caregiver for Mama, God made it happen by bringing Vern Jackson and his lovely wife Sandra into my life. Vern was my favorite singer on television.

Through the Jackson's, I was blessed with a job booking Vern into churches, and a standing invitation to open his concerts. Vern recorded my song, *Around Mama's Table* for his *Hello Mama* project. The album, to commemorate Mother's Day, was just one of the lovely things that was to happen that day. God's plan for *The Masterpiece* was about to be revealed.

Sandra Jackson's birthday was coming up, and while pondering what to give this elegant woman, the answer came: Give her the painting. Once again, Jesus would be a birthday gift. While the look of delight on Sandra's face was very pleasing, her words filled my heart with joy!

"The TV station has to have this! If you can get another one, Vern will see to it." You might be wondering, if it was that easy, why hadn't I asked Vern to handle it in the first place? Because then it would have been taken out of God's hands. He wasn't finished with this project yet. There were a few lessons to be learned about faith. The first stumbling block was the matter of the price of the second print of *The Masterpiece*. Although Bette Myers and her husband Marlin gave me a discount, it was money I didn't have. I knew they couldn't keep giving away Bette's beautiful painting, so once again, I settled down to wait upon the Lord to make a way. Months ago, I had booked a round of nine churches for Vern Jackson in Phoenix, Arizona, (where Bette lived) which should have simplified the matter of getting the extra painting. All I had to do was purchase it from Bette and Vern could take it with him. I called Bette every day, asking her to be patient. I was sure if God was in this, I would have the money before Vern ministered in the last church. Since Phoenix was also home for me, I'd brought Mama with me from Bakersfield and we attended every booking. By the time I introduced Vern at the eighth one, I still didn't have the money to buy the painting. Knowing from experience God sometimes answers at the last minute, I tried to keep the faith. Feeling a little discouraged I walked into the church lobby after the concert. It was then someone tapped me on the shoulder. I turned to see an attractive lady reaching into her purse.

"I have something for you from God," she said, "He said you would know what to do with it." Handing me a check for one hundred dollars, she frowned. "I don't know how God expects me to replace this money but I have to give it to you."

On Mother's Day, Vern appeared with Bette Myer's portrait of Jesus on live television. The next day Bette called to say the phone hadn't stopped ringing with orders for *The Masterpiece*. Marlin was returning my check. In turn, I sent it back to the lady who had given it to me! In the end, we were all blessed by the Birthday Gift.

MY FRIEND MARGARET , VERN AND SANDRA
JACKSON AND ME AT A PHOENIX CONCERT

THE LAST STOP

And let us not be weary in well doing

for in due season we shall reap,

if we faint not.

Gal.6:9

WEEKEND TRAVELERS SPED PAST me, as I sat in my car on the shoulder of Highway 99 in California. Lucky people, I thought with envy, they know their destination. As their twinkling taillights disappeared from my view, I put my head down on the steering wheel and gave in to the tears that threatened to fall for hours now. Looking for a tissue to dry my eyes, I decided. This is it, I'm going home! A singer by profession, I was opening for Vern Jackson, Gospel recording artist, on a ten day tour that I had booked myself, as his agent. I'd been driving in vain for an hour trying to find the church where we were appearing tonight. I'd left my copy of our itinerary on the coffee table back home in Bakersfield.

"What's the matter," asked my mother in the passenger seat. "Why are we stopping?" We had taken many trips together over the years and this was a first. I'd never pulled off the road in a display of tears before. Mom and I had followed the nightclub circuit for years, in search of our dream, to make me a recording artist. I had enjoyed some success, even making The Billboard Top100 Country Singles chart, but the job I had now was an answered prayer. Only this time, my mother, who used to walk so proudly beside me, was reduced to a wheel chair She, who so loved a good conversation, was now deaf. Her pretty hazel eyes, that had once never missed a trick, were almost blind. I studied her for moment, thinking how healthy she appeared. By looking at her you would never know that she was a total invalid. You couldn't detect it in her voice either, for it was as strong as ever, as she asked sharply, "Why are you crying?"

As I looked around in the seat for the dry-erase board that was my only means of communication with her, I remembered how excited I had been about this tour. Especially the last stop. While booking the churches over the telephone, I had somehow stumbled onto a church attended by a friend of the Jackson's whom they hadn't seen in a long time. Her name was Victoria. She'd made and gifted Vern with a beautiful leather jacket that he frequently wore on his television appearances. I wanted to be a part of their re-union, but it didn't look like I'd make it. Lost, I furiously scribbled on the board and handed it back to Mom. "That never stopped you before, go to a gas station and get directions." she ordered.

Tired! I wrote, handing the board back to her. Exhausted would have been closer to the truth. Repeatedly lifting my mother, who out-weighed me fifty pounds, in and out of the car, had finally taken its toll on me. Looking down at my rumpled suit, I wished I had another to change into, but new clothes were simply not in our budget. There was no money for hotels either. That's why we had to go home after each service, and start over again the next morning. "Tired is no excuse!" Mama responded in her usual direct way. Then, her sharp tone softening, she asked, "What about God, can't you do it for Him?"

I tried to ignore the concern in her voice, but my compassion won out. After all, she had cause to be concerned. If I crumpled, she would too; I was her only lifeline. While I pondered her question, God waited patiently. Press on, He whispered in my soul, I have gifts for you!

You see, God had a plan. He knew I needed friends. I'd left mine back in Arizona when I came to California to take care of my mother. And He knew the people up the road at the last stop. They were friends of Vern and Sandra Jackson. Dean, a soft-spoken gentleman who liked to take part in making peoples dreams come true and his lovely wife Victoria, known as

Tory, who delighted in giving. Yes, God looked ahead and saw a friendship that would endure through the years and not be diminished by time or distance. He surely must have smiled when He heard Mama say, "Well, what are you waiting for? Let's go find that church!"

In spite of the fact that we arrived too late to meet Dean and Tory at the concert, God already had his soldiers lined up. After the beautiful service at the church, Sandra Jackson insisted that I could not go home until I met Tory. She enlisted the aid of a friend to take Mama and me to Dean and Tory's lovely home. We all bonded instantly. Tory, a clothing designer with her own line of fabulous attire, took me to her beautiful dress shop, and treated me to a private shopping spree. What fun!

I felt like Cinderella, and as any woman would be, I was overjoyed to receive three, gorgeous new suits. And the best gift of all, my new-found friends!

Driving home to Bakersfield that night, I glanced over at Mama, asleep in the passenger seat. Thank God for her! I thought, re-living the day in my mind. If not for her motherly guidance, I might have given up today. Smiling to myself, I came to the same conclusion I always did. I needed her as much as she did me.

Since then, there have been other times when I've grown weary and wanted to quit, but I never do. I've learned to go the extra mile. The memory of that night spurs me on. I keep going because I can't wait to see what blessings He has for me, just up the road, at the last stop.

THIRTY MINUTES AGO

Then shalt thou call,

and the Lord shall answer:

Thou shalt cry and

He shall say, "Here I am."

Isaiah 58:9

FRUSTRATED, I HUNG UP the phone and stared at it for a minute in disappointment. Pushing my chair back from my desk, I got up to stretch my legs. I needed a break. Glancing at my watch as I rubbed my sore neck, I knew there was no time to spare. I was on a deadline and time was running out. I had been on the phone for hours now, and I only had one more hour to complete this project. A booking agent for Vern Jackson, a Gospel singer, who ministered in churches around the country; it was up to me to schedule him. Except for days like this, I loved my job. I'd been working for Vern several years now, and so far I'd been successful keeping him busy. If the church I was calling was familiar with the television network Vern appeared on, then the date was almost always a shoo-in. If not, I had to convince the music director to take a chance on a singer he'd never heard of. I had respect for Vern's talent and was usually able to convey that belief in such a way that they would feel they were missing a blessing, if they didn't book him. Believing this job had been a gift from the Lord, I took it seriously. Knowing Vern and Sandra trusted me, and not wanting to let them down, I pressed on until the last church on the tour was scheduled.

Sitting back down at my desk I put my head down on my arm and began to pray: Lord, I need you. Someone, somewhere in this town needs Vern Jackson to minister in their church and you know where they are. Please show me! Raising my head, a thought suddenly occurred to me: Look in the Yellow Pages.Normally, I worked from a church directory list; I hadn't checked the phone book for a while, but I would now!

Running my finger down the list of churches, I felt compelled to stop at one. I dialed the number and a woman answered. Our conversation, as I recall it, went like this:

"Hello, may I speak to the pastor, please?" "He's not here. What do you need?" she asked abruptly.

A little rebuffed by her tone, I began, "I represent Vern Jackson and,"

"We'll take him." she quickly interrupted me.

Surprised, I asked, "Wouldn't you like some information?" "Well, yes I would, but we'll take him."

"Are you the pastor's wife?" I asked, not quite believing this conversation.

"Yes, I am," she reported in her no-nonsense tone, "And I said, we'll take him!"

"You don't have to consult your husband?" I persisted.

"No, I don't, now tell me, when is Vern coming?"

After giving her the date and other information, I was feeling comfortable enough to ask, "Do you mind if I share something wonderful with you?"

"Shoot." she answered.

"Thirty minutes ago I prayed over the yellow pages and God told me to call you."

"Well, she responded, thirty minutes ago I was mopping the kitchen floor, praying for one of them television stars, like Vern Jackson, to come to our church." The service was a complete success. The pastor and his lovely wife went to great lengths to make it an unforgettable night. As for myself, I certainly won't forget the church God personally chose from the yellow pages in the phone book.

THE GOD CONNECTION

Psalms 37:4

Delight thyself also in the Lord

And He shall give thee

the desires of thine heart

S HE WAS THE LAST passenger to deplane Flight 283 from Oklahoma City to Phoenix, Arizona, where I waited, impatiently, to meet her. In fact, I had been waiting years for this glorious moment to arrive.

"Calm down, Honey." My husband Dick said, putting a hand on my shoulder. "You are shaking all over." In my excitement, I had fairly danced from one foot to the other in the hour and a half since we had arrived, early, at the airport. As she came closer into my vision I could hardly contain my joy. Here she comes, my favorite singer of all time, Jody Miller!

Almost holding my breath in anticipation, I watched the lovely, petite lady walking toward me, carrying her guitar, her shiny mahogany hair bouncing on her shoulders, as she briskly made her way through the crowd.

When finally, she stood smiling before me, I impulsively reached out and hugged her.

After all, I knew her much better than she did me. To me, she was a mentor and a major influence in my singing style, while to her, I was a fan she could now put a face on.

In awe, I stepped back and smiled at the woman who had achieved so much in her life. She had accomplished, in her musical career, what some singers only dream of.

But this story isn't about Jody Miller's many hit records, her numerous awards and accolades, including a Grammy, or even, her long black limousines. It's the story of how a friendship between two singers came about in an unsuspected way. One who had already achieved fame and the other struggling to attain it. It began, when I was young and trying to get into the music business. I had come in late one night to announce: "Mama, wake up, I've got great news!" "I went to a Jam Session tonight and sang Jody Miller's hit, *Queen of the House* and the band hired me!" "Get ready, Mama, we're going on the road." After a successful tour with a Country Western band, we came home and set out on our own. While Jody was winning awards and riding in limousines, Mama and I were driving our old Chevy looking for the big break We stopped at every dance club touting live music, with the hope I'd be discovered. One time she booked me into a club where the stage was decorated with chicken wire. When she realized that the wire was there to protect the band from flying bottles, she indignantly whisked me back out the door we had just come in. But not before a sharp dressing-down to the owner: "Why the very idea!" Mama bristled, "We don't even drink alcohol!" Jody Miller unknowingly accompanied us on the car radio, everywhere we went. Mama loved her singing and ranked her right up there with the King, a huge star. Mama, my self-appointed manager, held Jody up to me as a standard of excellence. She told me, "You could sing like that too, young lady, if you tried." When I attempted to tell her that I couldn't sing that high her solution was, "Well then, just sing lower."

And that's what I did for the next few years. While I landed jobs as a featured female vocalist and even sang for the troops in Viet Nam, the thrill of stardom eluded me. Finally, in Phoenix, Arizona, it happened! Not exactly the way Mama planned it, but it made me deliriously happy! I was discovered by the club owner who auditioned me. He turned out to be the love of my life. Dick and I married and I went on to sing at the Nite Life for almost twenty years. One day, Mama, who had moved back to California, called to ask about Jody Miller. I told her about the *Queen of the House* star appearing at a nearby venue, adding, "Isn't it ironic, our club is standing room only, so I can't attend Jody's concert." In the eighties, I had my fifteen minutes of fame by making the Billboard charts. I looked for her, but sadly, Jody Miller had disappeared. Eventually, I turned to gospel music and started a Christian booking agency while working for Vern Jackson Ministries. Mama, diagnosed with Alzheimer's now, was sleeping the day I went into the garage to sort through things stored there. Coming across some old record albums, I turned one over. Jody's pretty face smiled back at me. Memories of happier times floated back. Standing there among the boxes, the image of a young, vibrant mother played through my mind. It was Mama, years ago, eagerly turning up the volume on the car radio lest she miss a note of a Jody Miller song. *I'll Never meet her now*, I thought as I regretfully put the album back. But, as a believer, I shouldn't have under-estimated the power of God. Three days later I received a phone call that fulfilled a long-time hearts desire. The caller was Vern Jackson who told me Jody Miller's portfolio, as a new Christian artist, had fallen into his hands. Remembering that she was my favorite singer, he asked if I could help by booking her into some churches. Borrowing one of Vern's own phrases, I answered with enthusiasm: "It's a done deal!"

That commitment started a beautiful friendship between Jody and me. In time, I'd have the honor of opening some of her concerts and in turn she'd lend her beautiful voice to several songs I'd have a part in writing. *The Last Call to Supper* and *Liberty Man*.

Since the day we met at the airport, our mutual respect for each other - - - plus all the things we have in common - - - have carried us through the ups and downs that are part of all friendships. In good times or bad, it's a given we'll always be there for each other. But, it's our God connection that makes us sisters. Thanks to Him, and all the angels who got together and conspired to make a dream come true, Jody will always be the sister I never had, but always wanted.

PART 3:
JOURNEYS END

And blessed is she that believed:

for there shall be a performance

of those things which were

told her from the Lord.

Luke 1:45

NO GOODBYES

Once upon another time

we'll meet again

Another place and time

Our story will begin . . .

B. Belt

"GRACIE, COME HERE!" My mother called out to me as I walked past the couch where she sat. It broke my heart, as always, to hear her address me by my aunt's name. The Alzheimer's disease that the doctor had warned me about several years ago seemed to have finally set in. My mother didn't know me anymore. In spite of doing all I could to trigger her memory, even writing my name Bonnie in big letters on the dry-erase board which was our only means of communication, it had been weeks now since she had known me. After a lifetime of conversations, and a close relationship, it hurt me terribly to think that I was wiped out of her thoughts entirely.

"Gracie, go find Bonnie for me, I must talk to her!" she gripped my hand tightly when I walked over to find out what she wanted. Helplessly, I looked into her tear-filled eyes, wishing she had asked for something simple, like a glass of water. Four years ago I had put my life on hold to take care of her and so far I had managed to grant her every wish. I had learned to cook the old-fashioned food that she craved, such as wilted lettuce which sounded so simple, but I hadn't a clue how to make, and somehow had found the strength to lift her into the car, for what seemed like the millionth time, to take her for that daily ride that she enjoyed so much.

Legally blind, totally deaf, and unable to walk after two broken hips, she was getting more and more difficult to care for at home. Still, I just couldn't bring myself to put her in a nursing home. Besides wanting to keep my promise to my mother (it now seemed like a hundred years ago) that she could stay with me, I felt I had to honor the promise that I'd made to God, when I was a child, to always take care of her.

It was to Him that I called silently now, as I watched the tears pouring down her face. My strong little Mama, who rarely cried, was sobbing in earnest, "Please, Gracie, find Bonnie for me! I need to tell her something important!" Gently, I loosened her fingers from around my wrist and went into my bedroom.

Dropping to my knees beside my bed, I began to pray: Lord, she needs me so. Please, God, just let her know me for a few minutes! As I continued praying and thanking Him for all the answered prayers He'd already given me, I began to feel a gentle peace washing over me. Walking back into the room where I had left her crying such a short time ago, I marveled at the transformation in her. The tears had disappeared and her little face was wreathed in smiles. Her hazel eyes, usually dull and cloudy, sparkled like emeralds and were lit up in bright recognition as she exclaimed excitedly, "Bonnie, you've come!" Sweet relief flooded my heart as I sat down beside her and took her hand. "Bonnie, you'll never know how glad I am to see you. I have wanted to talk to you for a long time!" She squeezed my hand and continued all in one breath, "Are you still working for the Jackson's ? Oh, what grand people," she added with a smile.

As I turned and picked up the dry-erase board to write my answer, she unexpectedly pushed it away. "Oh, we won't need that thing today," she said emphatically. "I can hear!" I looked at her in amazement and she repeated slowly, with emphasis on each word: "I- can -hear -you." She looked at me and smiled, "Isn't God wonderful?"

She folded her hands in her lap. "Remember that old song you used to sing to me when you were little? I think it was called . . ." She hesitated, put her hand to her head, and appealed, "You'll have to forgive my memory." Then suddenly and triumphantly, she announced, *Scarlet Ribbons*." "Now Bonnie," she went on in her old voice of authority, "I believe you should put our story in writing and make a recording of that song. I've got a good feeling about it. Will you do that for me?"

Would I do that for her? My wonderful mother whose love and support had paved the way for me to become a professional singer. Yes, Mama, a lonely voice inside me cried out to her, I would do anything for you! Unable to speak, my throat so constricted with emotion, I could only nod in reply. Bowing my head onto my chest, I whispered, "Oh Mom, I love you so!" In that moment, it seemed a miracle had taken place, for she answered as if she had heard me, "I know, Bonnie, I love you too." As I raised my head in surprise, she saw my tears. "Don't cry, no goodbyes, we'll meet again, you know." But it was her next words to me that hit my heart the hardest. Words, that with a sudden flash of foresight, I knew I'd never hear again. She had said them to me in parting since I was a child. Reaching over to pat my cheek, she said, "You be good now!"

Overcome with emotion, I had to leave the room. When I came back, the sparkle had left her eyes and the dull, confused look had returned, "What's for lunch Gracie?" But I wasn't upset. After years of prayer to God, to restore my mother's hearing, I believe He finally opened her ears. Her last comment was like music to my own when she smiled and said, "Thank you, Gracie, for finding Bonnie. She was here you know!"

THE HOUSE FAITH BOUGHT

Trust in the Lord with all thine heart;

Lean not unto thine own understanding.

In all thy ways acknowledge Him and

He shall direct thy paths.

Proverbs 3:5,6

S TANDING AT THE STOVE, stirring the soup I was making, the eerie wail of an ambulance, in the distance, took me back to a recent night when it stopped at my own door. Mama had unexpectedly suffered a massive stroke while I was caring for her. Within minutes my house was a scene of bedlam as paramedics worked frantically to save her. At the hospital, doctors held out no hope she would live. They advised me to start making funeral arrangements. Instead, I went to church and prayed. Two weeks later the staff was calling her The Miracle Lady. Tomorrow she was coming home!

Home held different meanings for both of us. Her idea was the small town of Taft, California, where she'd lived most of her life, and mine was here in Phoenix, Arizona. I'd brought her back here several months ago, but every day she begged to go home. She was deaf and I couldn't make her understand, Taft was not an option. The only family living there was her sister's daughter, Marie, (nick-named Punkie) who was Mama's favorite niece. While I knew Punkie would take her in if she could, her house was much too small to accommodate Mama. The tiny cottage was crowded enough with Punkie's sister and daughter living there. As a last resort, I'd checked the nursing home, but it had a long waiting list. The only answer was a rest home in Bakersfield. Continuing to stir the soup, I began to pray. Lord, my heart is breaking! You know I don't want to take her to Bakersfield. Please show me what to do! Turning the burner off under the soup pot, I heard the words: Take her to Taft. My first instinct was to argue with that little voice, after all, I knew there was no place for her there, but thinking of a scripture I'd read recently about God's ways being higher than ours, I decided to trust Him. Now, all I had to do was convince my husband Dick I was doing the right thing.

Later, over a bowl of soup, I broke the news to Dick. "There's been a slight change of plans," I told him. "We're taking Mama to Taft."

"Where did you get that idea?" he asked with a puzzled look.

"God." I answered, waiting for an outburst from him. Surprisingly, Dick agreed.

"Well, He's never steered you wrong before so why would He now? When do we leave?" Dick asked with a cheerful smile. The next morning, unbeknownst to me at the time, God began orchestrating His plan. Since He was in charge of my finances and knew who owed me money, He sent them to my door with cash. By mid-day, I had four-hundred dollars tucked away in my wallet!

Dick, who liked driving at night, picked us up that evening and we set out for the five hundred mile trip to Taft. When we arrived, the weather had changed and it was pouring rain. Dick, chivalrous gentleman he was, wrapped Mama in a blanket and carried her in the house. I hadn't let Punkie know we were coming, but if she was surprised she didn't show it. I knew she was probably wondering why we were there, while welcoming us with open arms. Not sure where to begin, I blurted out to her, "God sent us." Punkie, without hesitation, smiled and said, "Let's talk." Explaining my dilemma concerning Mama, I was reminded of a story in the Bible about there being no room for baby Jesus at the Inn. At that moment, Punkie's teen-age daughter, Dee-Dee, getting ready for school, suddenly bounded into the room. After hugging us she announced: "I have the answer to your problem!"

Exchanging dubious glances, but curious to know her solution, we let her speak. "There's a house up the street for sale. It's big enough for all of us. You can buy it!"

At a loss for words, wondering how to explain to this enthusiastic young girl what buying a house involved, I let her go on, her pretty green eyes shining with excitement.

"The house belongs to me. I've already laid hands on it and claimed it for my family!" Without missing a beat. she added, "Don't you see? It's the answer!" Moving us into a circle where we all joined hands, she began to pray out loud. While she petitioned the Lord on our behalf, the end of another scripture flashed through my mind . . . and a little child shall lead them. Ending her prayer with a fervent amen, she said earnestly, "Now, I'm going to school and when I get home at three o'clock I am expecting the key to our new house." With that said, she picked up her books and walked out the door. As we stepped out on the tiny front porch to watch her walking down the sidewalk, blonde ponytail swinging, she suddenly turned back and said, "Don't worry guys, I've got you covered, I have enough faith for all of you!"

Back in the living room, we stared at each other in stunned silence, until Dick reached for his jacket and said, "We'd better go take a look at Dee-Dee's dream house."

The house, built in the nineteen forties, wore a fresh coat of white paint, and the tree in the front yard gave the place a homey look. Deep steps led up to a wide veranda built across the front of the house. Even with the rain pelting down on my umbrella, I visualized potted plants, an old fashioned swing, and pitchers of lemonade being served on that porch. Wanting to see the back yard, we were going around the side of the house, when a car pulled up in front and a stocky man carrying a clip-board got out and walked toward us. Wondering how he'd known we were here when we hadn't even called yet, we introduced ourselves. We asked Fred to show us the inside of the house.

The bedrooms were large, it had a nice kitchen and a charming dining room with a built in mahogany china cabinet. Punkie, who liked the out-doors, would appreciate the back yard with roses already in bloom. After the tour, we understood why Dee-Dee loved the house so much. We wanted it for her, but the owner wouldn't give us a price. Every time the cost was brought up, Fred would show us some minor repair that was needed and say he was knocking five-hundred off. He wrote everything down on his clip-board. Finally, an hour later he told us he'd gotten the price down to under forty thousand and asked us to come to his house to do the paperwork. We agreed to meet him after lunch. Discussing our morning over grilled cheese sandwiches Dick and I decided the whole thing would be comical if the house wasn't so important to us. But, the strangest part was yet to come.

When we arrived at Fred's house, he greeted us as if we were old friends. He told me of taking care of his own mother and how he respected me for what I was trying to do for mine. Then he said something that struck me as odd. "I know you have four hundred dollars and I'll trade you for these." He reached in his pocket and pulled out a set of keys and laid them on his desk. Handing me his clip-board he said, "Now you look these disclosures over and decide if you want the house." Dick and I both read it, but there was nothing listed except for a missing smoke detector and a few light bulbs. I know the man was real, we made four-hundred dollar payments on that house for years, but in that moment he seemed to me like an angel from God! We were ten minutes late getting back to Punkie's house and Dee-Dee was in her room doing home-work. She looked up at us expectantly, and Dick, with the glint of a tear in his eye, threw her the keys. We all started to laugh and cry at the same time. By nightfall, we had the beds moved and made up. Mama had her own room. She passed away there a few months later. She went peacefully in her sleep, at home, in the house faith bought.

TO MAMA WITH LOVE

Love bears all things, believes all things,

hopes all things. Love never fails.

1 Cor.13:7, 8

THE STREETS OF BAKERSFIELD were dear and familiar to me, driving through them on my way to the airport. Familiar, since I'd spent several years here as Mama's care-giver and dear because they represented the good times we'd had together. Years that turned out to be mother's last, yet brought us more happiness than we could have imagined. Mama, who had been given three days to live when I came here, had out-lived the doctors' grim prognosis by more than three years. It was as if God had temporarily called a halt to her illness. She seemed to flourish with each new day. Always a good sport, she was ready for any challenge that came our way. And, there were a few!

As for myself, instead of having to put my singing career on the back burner while I cared for Mama, God had opened doors and given me a music ministry I loved. He sent His angels to guide me, answered all my prayers and gave me the desires of my heart. I held this town in reverence because I felt God's presence with us constantly.

Today, I was back in Bakersfield for one reason. I'd come back to California to honor my mother's final wishes. Toward the end of her life Mama was stricken with Alzheimer's Disease. But God had given Mama a moment of respite from the illness clouding her mind so she could talk to me. In a flash of clarity she made a last request. After telling me to write our story, she asked me to make a recording of *Scarlet Ribbons*. The song I'd been singing to her since I was eight years old.

While I couldn't imagine why she wanted this done - - - when she wouldn't be here to enjoy it - - - she said, "I've got a good feeling about it!" That was enough reason for me. In the years we'd been chasing dreams together, following Mama's intuition always led to something better. Knowing she still supported my singing, despite her illness, meant so much to me, I was determined to make it happen. Fortunate enough to line up Buck Owens band for a recording session, today I'd sing Mama's favorite song once again. Arriving from Oklahoma City was our favorite recording artist, Jody Miller. As soon as she heard about my plan to carry out Mama's last wish, Jody volunteered to help out on the session. We learned later that Buck Owens said if he'd known Jody was going to be there, he would have been delighted to play some rhythm guitar. Mama would have been impressed! She was a big fan of Buck's. But she would've been more excited over the appearance of her girl, Jody Miller. We'd been fans of the award winning singer since her song, *Queen of the House*, became a smash hit. Through the years Jody would have dozens of chart records to her credit. Her songs got a lot of air-play on radio stations and every time her voice came on the car radio, Mama reached over and turned up the volume. When the song ended she'd declare, "Someday, we're going to meet Jody Miller, you mark my words!"

Strangely, Mama was right. Except for one thing: She wouldn't be included in the long anticipated meeting. When I first met Jody and told her how much her singing meant to Mama, she wanted to meet her right away. Jody and I drove the five-hundred mile trip to the little town of Taft to see her, but sadly, Mama was too far gone to even know Jody was in the room. Mama never met her favorite singer, but she'd have her victory even in death. Her beloved Jody Miller was going to the studio with me today to sing harmony to *Scarlet Ribbons*. I believed Mama would be there, if only in spirit. Jody was waiting at the curb when I pulled up at the airport. Putting her guitar into the back seat, she smiled, "Well, are we going to make some music for Mama or what?" On our way we saw a fast-food place, and Jody said, "Let's stop for a hot dog, okay?" I didn't have the heart tell her it was where I used to buy them for Mama. "Sounds good to me," I answered, pulling over to park. When I started to get out of the car, Jody pressed me back and insisted, "Let me, I'll go and get them."

I couldn't help thinking, *Oh, if Mama could only see me now, her famous Jody Miller buying me a hot dog!* I silently thanked God for my good fortune. Now, riding to the studio in comfortable silence, both of us lost in our own thoughts, I realized that my journey's end was in sight. In a few hours it would be over and this town would become a beautiful memory. I'd done all I could for Mama and kept my promise to God. I was free to go home where my husband, Dick, patiently waited. But, first, there was Mama's last request to fulfill. Walking into the studio with Jody, I had to smile. Years ago, listening to her on the radio, who would have thought she and I would be here in Bakersfield, recording a song together. I could almost hear Mama saying, in her forth-right way, "Only God could have pulled that one off!"

Putting on my headphones, I waited for the opening chords of the beloved old song to sound in my ears. Dedicating it to Mama with love, I began to sing *Scarlet Ribbons.*

ONCE UPON
ANOTHER TIME

I waited patiently for the Lord

And He heard my cry

And He set my foot upon a rock

and established my goings.

Ps. 40:2

ONLY 45 SHOPPING DAYS 'til Christmas" read the caption on the bottom of the news- paper I was reading, on a rainy day in November.

The last thing I wanted to think about now was the holiday season. I was alone, my only child was living many miles away and worst of all, I had lost my beloved mother four months earlier.

Please Lord, I began to pray, Help me get through this holiday season. Send me a job and please God, send my husband back to me. A few minutes passed and a strange thought occurred to me: Look at yesterdays paper you threw away. As I pulled the discarded, pencil marked, help wanted section out of the trash, an ad jumped out at me. It read: We need your smiling face! Work in a fun, happy atmosphere! I sighed, trying to remember the last time I'd had fun. I hadn't been to a party or even a movie for the last four years. My whole world was wrapped up in my mother, an invalid who needed constant care. She lived in California and my home was in Arizona. When she first became ill, I was constantly traveling between the two states to care for her. Finally, her condition worsened and it became necessary for me to take up residence with her. Dick and I'd had a successful marriage for over twenty years and separating was painful for both of us. Now, with Mama gone and circumstances different, I imagined we would just fall into each other's arms and pick up where we left off. After all, we still loved each other. But, the reconciliation wasn't happening the way I dreamed of. Living apart for so long had taken its toll on our relationship. Still, I prayed for our reunion. Thinking of Dick now, the thought I'd had earlier came to my mind again, look at yesterdays paper you threw away! Smoothing out the wrinkled newspaper, I dialed the number in the ad. To my surprise, I was asked to come for an interview that day. The position, a receptionist in a ballroom dance studio, was intriguing. A professional singer myself, when it came to dancing, I had two left feet. Fortunately, the job only required office experience. I was hired on the spot to work at the front desk.

Three weeks later, a co-worker handed me a paper to fill out. It was a Christmas Wish List from my employer. "Oh no, I told Michelle, I can't put anything down, I've worked here less than a month. The owner barely knows me."

"Yes you can, Michelle insisted, write down several things you really want and the boss will buy them for you!"

Feeling somewhat unworthy, I filled out the list and included my favorite perfume. When the day of the party finally arrived and my husband, Dick called un-expectedly. I invited him to accompany me to the Christmas Gala. Greeted with warm, welcoming smiles when we arrived, Dick and I sat down to enjoy the music and watch the young dancers whirl their partners around the floor. Intimidated by their intricate moves, Dick and I decided not to embarrass ourselves trying to compete. But the couples' friendly overtures encouraged us to, at least, give it a try. Thankfully it was a waltz, the only dance steps we knew. At home in each others arms, caught up in the lyrics of the tune, the embers of our lingering love sparked up. Fittingly, the song playing was, *Could I Have This Dance (For the Rest of My Life)*.

After dinner the presents were distributed. I was amazed at the pile in front of me. Every gift on my list was there, even the perfume. I smiled my thanks at the lovely woman who'd made this night possible. A champion dancer herself, she was the boss. Our marriage restored, Dick and I went on to share more happy holidays, but the one that stands out in my memory, like a single shining star, is that lonely time in my life when God used a crumpled piece of newspaper, out of the trash, to answer my prayers!

ALL THE COWS
ON THE HILLS

For every beast in the forest is mine,

And the cattle on a thousand hills

Ps.50:10

I WOKE UP ON THAT May morning with a feeling that something wonderful was about to happen. Then I remembered it was Mother's Day and someone special was sleeping in our guest room. The person was my long-time singing mentor, Jody Miller.

I smiled to think how she came to be in my life. She had been a household name at the time Mama and I became her fans. Her hit song, *Queen of the House* was played on the radio so often, I knew the words by heart. A singer myself, I sang the catchy tune with a band one night, and was hired on the spot. Thanks to Jody's recording of that song, she won a Grammy Award and I went on to a long career as a country vocalist.

While I never achieved the fame Jody had, I wasn't envious. At one time I had a chance for a recording career, but turned to writing inspirational music instead. This opened the door to become a booking agent for Gospel singer, Vern Jackson, who called me one day with Jody Miller's phone number. She too, was now singing for the Lord. I still remember how excited I was when Dick and I met her at the airport for the first time. But that was a year ago and since then Jody and I had become very good friends. Today, a church in Kingman was going to be blessed with her singing. I was going with her, and Dick wanting to do something nice for us on our special day, was renting a new car for the three hour drive there. Dick had another idea while I was getting ready.

"Honey, why don't you ask Jody to let you sing today?"

"No, Dear, I can't do that," I answered, looking for my pink lipstick. "But, it's Mothers Day and you could sing *Scarlet Ribbons*," he insisted.

"If she wanted to share the stage with me, I assured him, she'd ask me herself." Seeing the disappointed look on his face, I relented. "I'll ask God to handle it, okay?"

"Okay," he answered, turning away with a skeptical look, "But if He doesn't, I will!"

A familiar old song from the Sixties was playing on the car radio when Jody and I drove to the rental agency to pick up the new car. We were ecstatic when presented with a holiday special. A beautiful, lavender Lincoln Town Car for the price of a compact! Jody drove my car on the ten minute drive back to the house to pick up our things and say goodbye to Dick When we pulled in the driveway, Jody, getting out of my car asked "Bonnie, do you have a soundtrack of the music for *Scarlet Ribbons?*"

"Yes, I do," I answered, marveling how God answers prayers so quickly.

"Good!" Jody responded, "I want you to open my concert today." Dick, standing out front waiting for us, heard her and said, "I know right where it is."

When we arrived at the church, Jody asked the pastor to introduce me first. I told the congregation how many years Mama and I had been Jody Miller fans. I told them how God brought Jody into my life. That Jody had gone with me to see Mama for the last time. How sad we felt when she didn't recognize us, and how we prayed that somehow, she'd know we were there. Expressing my sorrow that my mother didn't live to share this beautiful day, I sang her favorite song, *Scarlet Ribbons*. When Jody appeared and gave her own heart-felt testimony, her beautiful, melodic voice ringing out in praise to Him, the whole church was blessed. She brought me back to share her standing ovation.

After the concert we stopped for a nice dinner and Jody wanted to drive the Lincoln back to Phoenix. While discussing the lovely service, I finally asked her the question burning in my mind. "Jody, what prompted you to invite me to sing today?" "Simple," she stated. "It was the car radio. That station you have on in your car played *Scarlet Ribbons* and I remembered that you sang it to your mother." "But, Jody," I protested, "I've listened to that station for years. They play a lot of old music but they've never, ever, played *Scarlet Ribbons!*"

"Well, she said smiling, they played it today and I'm glad they did!" Later that evening when Dick and I were alone, I told him why Jody asked me to sing.

"What are the chances of that happening? he asked. Our car radios have been tuned to that station for over twenty years and we never heard the song Today, God had a ten minute window of time to get the job done and He did!" "God works in mysterious ways His wonders to perform," Dick said, smiling. "Remember the scriptures you read to me about Him owning all the silver and gold and the cows on the hills?" Amused at the cow part (the scripture read cattle) I encouraged my darling husband to continue.

"It makes sense to me, Dick went on, if He owns all that, He owns the radio stations too. He can play any song He wants to!" Laughing, I agreed with him. You see, I didn't care how Dick reasoned it out in his head, I just wanted to make sure he was giving God all the glory.

That day opened the door to many more shared concerts with Jody. We went on to become friends for life. Exactly the way God planned when He brought two singers together, and sealed their friendship with a song!

JODY MILLER RECORDING MY SONG LIBERTY MAN

SCOOBY

(The Dog Faith Won)

Mark 11:24

Therefore I say unto you

When you pray, believe that you receive them

And ye shall have them

O N A BEAUTIFUL SATURDAY morning in May, I heard my husband Dick leaving the house. For a man who worked the night-shift to be up this early was unusual, so I hurriedly donned my robe and raced to the front door. "Where are you going?" I questioned,

"I'm going to get Scooby." He replied with a smile. "And I want to be first in line." Noticing the collar and lead in his hand that had once been worn by our Great Dane, Shadrach, I suddenly remembered. Scooby, titled Pet of The Week in the Arizona newspaper was up for adoption today at the Arizona Humane Society. Remembering our last conversation about it, I was surprised he was even going.

In our twenty years of marriage, we'd always had dogs to complete our family. Our newest member was Lady, a gentle, fawn Great Dane whom Dick rescued when he bought her from a family who had to keep her in a closet. Dick thought she might be lonely so he'd been trying to find a mate for her. One day, when he complained he hadn't been successful, I asked him, "Have you tried God?"

"No, I hadn't thought of that." He grinned. "Seriously, I continued, He can find the perfect dog if you ask Him. And remember, when you pray, believe that you receive." I was referring to my favorite Bible scripture.

About a week later Dick brought a newspaper clipping to me. "What do you think of him?" He asked, pointing to a picture of a dog being advertised for adoption. Knowing virtually nothing about the breed, which we later learned was English Mastiff, I said truthfully. "I think there will be a long line of people there to adopt him, possibly hundreds!" (Scooby had also been featured on a weekly television show)

For a moment my faith wavered. When I'd told him to pray for a dog, I certainly hadn't considered that he would choose one with so many obstacles. Kissing me goodbye, Dick said, "Please don't leave the house, I'm going to need help when I get Scooby home."

Wow, I thought, he certainly took me at my word when I told him to believe. But not wanting him to be disappointed if it wasn't to be, I said, "If you don't get Scooby, please look at the other dogs there."

With a patient look he replied, "I'm not going for another dog, I'm going for Scooby." "If God wants us to have him, he's already ours." He waved and drove away.

When the phone rang several hours later, I was elated to hear Dick's jubilant voice, "I won!" "They gave me and several hundred others a number and mine was drawn." "I'm bringing Scooby home!"

While the huge English Mastiff is the most loveable dog we've ever had, we also consider him to be a special gift from God. Scooby is a constant reminder that all things are possible to those who believe.

FAVOR

And be ye kind to one another.

Tenderhearted, forgiving one another,

as God hath forgiven you.

Eph. 4:32

Isn't that the way it always goes, I thought, impatiently, When you're in a hurry, you can never catch a green light! I was anxious to get back to the hospital to check on my husband, Dick, who had suffered a stroke just this morning. While waiting for a green light, I relived in my mind the terrible events that had happened early this morning.

At six I'd heard Dick getting out of bed. Too sleepy to get up myself, though I usually accompanied him everywhere since his health began to fail, I watched him through half-closed lids as he started toward the bathroom. Suddenly, he lurched to the right and started to fall. Oh, no, he's going to hit his head on the dresser! Frantically, I struggled to sit up. Then, as if a hand had reached out and pulled him back, he straightened up again. But only for a second. From what I could make out in the dimly lit room, he was going down. Waiting to hear a thud, instead, I heard a yelp from our dog. Thankfully, Scooby was lying by the bed, right where he needed to be. The huge English Mastiff broke his master's fall.

I barely remember calling 911 and waking my son Scotty who had moved back home to help after Dick's recent heart surgery. It wasn't until I was hurrying out the door to follow the ambulance that I realized Scotty was frightened too. "Mom," he cried out, pulling me aside, "It's all my fault, the argument that Dad and I had last night must have caused this!" The look of distress on his face tore at my heart. No mother can bear to see her child hurting, even after that child is all grown up. With no time to console him, I reached out and enveloped my six foot five son in a quick hug.

At the hospital Dick was diagnosed with a mild stroke. As soon as he was stable I went home to reassure Scotty that Dad was going to be alright. Still visibly upset, my son blamed himself for his step-dad's stroke. I did my best to convince him that their argument hadn't brought it on, that Dad's health had worsened since his heart attack. I could see by the look in his eyes that he had doubts, but I had to get back to the hospital.

Now, coming to another red light, I had time to think about their relationship. It was a stormy one. Constantly engaging in verbal battles, they just couldn't agree on anything. In spite of Dick's giving heart, he had a stubborn streak and sometimes wouldn't speak to Scotty for days after one of their arguments. Neither one wanted to be the first to give in and apologize. Stuck in the middle of their ever-widening rift, I didn't know what to do. Siding with one would surely hurt the other, and so I tried to remain neutral. Ten minutes away from the hospital, according to the car clock, I started my prayer. It was a very specific one. From the depths of my breaking heart, I cried out to Him,

Favor, Father, I ask you for favor! Let there be peace between the two people I love most. Forgive them Father God, and let them forgive each other. Now, please, Father, grant this request now. Not next month, not next year, I need it today!

Arriving at the hospital, the combination of antiseptics and rubbing alcohol assailed my nose as I stepped out of the elevator on the fifth floor. As I hurried toward Dick's room, a nurse behind a long desk asked, "Do you have a son?" "Yes I do."

"Is his name Scotty?" "Why?" I questioned, wondering if something had happened to him.

"Your husband's asking for him. He started calling for Scotty ten minutes ago."

My mind flashed back to the stoplight where I'd been praying ten minutes ago, and I knew the healing had begun. God had heard my prayer. Two weeks later, Scotty, wanting to do something nice for his Dad, took it upon himself to take Dick's beloved dog, Scooby, to visit him at the rehabilitation center. The simple act of kindness on Scotty's part sparked a kindred bond between them and won Dick's heart. An animal lover, Dick's motto was, "love me, love my dog," and that was one thing he and Scotty couldn't disagree on, they both loved Scooby. That was the beginning of the good things Scotty found to do for his Dad. Dick reciprocated by treating him like a man. A man he admired. Their mutual respect continued to grow until their relationship was as solid as a rock. They truly became the father and son I always wanted them to be.

When I remember that day, waiting for the green traffic lights, I wonder if God used all the red ones to stop me, so I could take time to pray for favor. A prayer He lovingly answered, and in doing so, changed our lives forever.

IN THE BLINK OF AN EYE

Then touched He their eyes saying,

According to your faith

Be it unto you

Matt.9:29

ALF-WAY HOME, I PULLED my car over to the side of the road. I couldn't make it another block. Something was terribly wrong with my right eye. It felt like it was on fire! The pain was excruciating. It started earlier at work and had grown steadily worse as the day wore on. Finally, I had to cancel the rest of my day and leave. Fumbling now in my purse for my cell phone, I suddenly remembered in my hurry to leave, I had left it on my desk, I was on my own. Glancing in my rear view mirror, I could barely see the blurry headlights of the cars behind me. I couldn't sit here all night waiting for my husband to find me. Frightened at the thought, I leaned back on the head rest and asked God to lead me safely home. Feeling calmer now, I pulled out into the traffic, driving in the far right lane. It was the longest ten miles of my life, but eventually, I made it home.

My husband Dick was standing in the driveway, a concerned look on his face. He'd called my office and when they told him I 'd left for home over an hour ago, he'd begun to worry. Seeing the state I was in, he said, "I'm taking you to the Emergency Room."

All the way there I sat on the passenger side of the car, rocking in pain. When we arrived, I was taken in to see a physician immediately. Dick went in with me. The doctor, shining a light in my eye, gave a little whistle and said to Dick, "Come here and take a look at this cut on her eye. No wonder she's in such pain. She'll have to see a specialist first thing in the morning!" Applying magic drops in my eye which instantly stopped the pain, he asked, "How did this happen?" "I might have gotten too close to a piece of paper, I answered, suddenly wary of the roll of gauze in his hand. When he put a big patch over my eye and proceeded to wrap the bandage around my head, I protested anxiously. "Oh no, Doctor, I can't wear this, I have to go back to work tomorrow and it just wouldn't match my . . . outfit . . . " My attempt at humor trailed off as he stepped back and folded his arms across his chest. But I was serious. I worked in a glamorous atmosphere at a ballroom dance studio and I dressed to the nines. There was no way I could greet a client looking like this!

"Well, the doctor said sternly, you have to wear a bandage. We're not dealing with a mere scratch. That cut has to be treated by a specialist and he will advise you what has to be done."

When we got home, Dick, treating me like an invalid, settled me in our guest room. "Try to relax now, he said tenderly. You've had a hard day. I'm going to fix you some dinner and then you can get some rest."

Smiling at his solicitous manner, I reminded him, "But you can't cook," "I think I can manage a bowl of soup, he said cheerfully. Where's the can opener?"

Anxious to be alone, so I could talk to God, I finished the soup in record time. When Dick turned off the light, assuring me that he would be right in the next room, I began to pray. I reminded God that I hadn't missed a day of work in seven years, and although I'd never been commended for it, it was to me, an important accomplishment. I told Him about recently being promoted to manager, a position that held many responsibilities and I had to be on the job to carry them out. Then, I started pleading with Him:

Father, You gave me this job and I've been faithful! I believe that You can just touch me and my eye will be healed. Please, do this for me now! I had been holding my hand on my bandaged eye as I prayed and suddenly a strange thing happened. For a few seconds I felt an intense heat penetrating my eye and then as quickly as it came, it was gone. But in my heart I knew, that I knew, what I knew!

Jumping out of bed, I ran to the family room where Dick was watching television and declared, "My eye has been healed! I'm going to work tomorrow." And I told him about my experience.

Turning off the television to give me his undivided attention, Dick said kindly, "Honey, I know you have a lot of faith, but remember, I saw that cut and there's simply no way it could heal that fast." "I really think you should wait and see what the specialist has to say. Now, what do you say we get some rest?" The next morning I was up early and ready for work, down to my three inch high heels, by the time Dick got up. "Good morning Beautiful," he greeted me, (after thirty years of marriage) "Where are you going all dressed up?"

"To work, as soon as I get this pirate patch off."

"Oh, Honey, you're too much!" he laughed. "At least you'll impress the doctor." The optometrist turned out to be a woman She put me at ease right away when she began to take off the bandage, saying, "Let's get this off, it doesn't match your outfit." Shining her light into my eye, she made an un-intelligible sound. My heart froze, what did that mean? I wondered, holding my breath in suspense. "Hmmm…" she murmured, looking into my eye a second time. Turning off her light, she was silent for a nerve-racking minute before stating, "I don't like to dispute another doctor's diagnosis, but I can't find one thing wrong with your eye."

I could have hugged her I was so happy! Wanting to share the moment, I looked over at Dick, who was smiling ear to ear, giving me the thumbs up sign. When we reached the privacy of our car, Dick exclaimed, "Either this is a huge coincidence, or you just got a miracle!"

"Well, you saw the cut in my eye, what do you think?"

"I think this whole experience has made a believer out of me." He answered.

I smiled to myself, thankful that some of my faith rubbed off on my husband!

A few days later a woman came to the studio. One of the job interviews I had to cancel the day I left early. Inviting her to sit down, I reached for an application form.

Waving it away, she said, "I was just passing by and felt the need to speak to you." "When your secretary called to cancel my interview, she told me you had to leave due to an eye injury. I wanted to commiserate with you because several months ago, I, too, had a cut on my eye. Mine took a long time to heal, and I was in my doctor's office several times a week. It turned out to be an expensive ordeal." "But you look fine." She said, giving me a closer inspection. "I guess I was more fortunate than you, for I had the best medical help available."

"Oh!" she said, her interest perking up, "Who was the doctor?"

"God." I answered, waiting for her response.

She said nothing, but her nod spoke volumes. Smiling, she stood up and was gone.

I never had the pleasure of meeting her again but I've always felt it was not by circumstance that she appeared that day. I believe she was sent to share her story so I might see what the consequences could have been. A confirmation, that by my faith, He healed me in the blink of an eye.

SANDRA'S SHOES

Love is pure and sacred

Like a golden wedding ring

Love is a one-time, Love is an all-time

Love is a lifetime thing

B. Belt

THE FIRST TIME I saw Sandra I had no idea what an important role she would play in my life. All I knew was that I wanted her for a friend, and I remember saying a little prayer that she would like me. I had come into her life quite unexpectedly when her husband Vern Jackson recorded a song that Id written for his *Hello Mama* album. This led to a job working for their ministry as a booking agent. Although I had never done this kind of work before, I gave it my all because I held these people in such high esteem. A singer myself, they let me open Vern's concerts and never seemed to mind when I brought Mama in her wheelchair. They made us feel like part of their family and my mother adored them. She always referred to the Jackson's as grand people.

When I returned to Phoenix after Mama passed away, Vern and Sandra came there once a year to minister at churches in the area. Vern Jackson was so well liked that the churches booked him back year after year. Dick and I looked forward to being with them. They always came bearing gifts chosen by Sandra. She unknowingly out-did herself the day she surprised my husband with a present of his own. White, canvas deck shoes which Dick promptly dubbed Sandra's shoes. Ordinary shoes that would become extraordinary because of the different meanings they would hold for both of us.

During the next year Dick's health began to fail, and I was devastated when doctors diagnosed him with Alzheimer's Disease. Armed with all the information I could find about it, I was determined to stay one step ahead of this dreadful illness. I planned daily activities to stimulate his thinking process.

We watched game shows on television and I encouraged Dick to participate. He was so happy when he could answer the hundred dollar question. We reminisced about his Navy days. Having written down everything he'd ever told me, I challenged him for the answers to: What was the name of his ship and where was he stationed? Oh, he loved to talk about, what he called, his Glory Days. Dick had been born into a large family and we could spend hours naming each one of his seven aunts and two uncles and then start on their children. Of course we never left out his daughter, Sheila and her three children. Everything he remembered that had happened recently was a cause for celebration. But the thing he seemed not to forget was Sandra's shoes. Every morning when I helped him dress he would ask me to put them on him. This request was like a symbol of hope to me that perhaps we could stop this terrible thing that was happening to us. But, unfortunately, there is no stopping Alzheimer's Disease. I learned that it is a progressive disease that can lead to death in seven to ten years or sometimes in four or five. My daily prayer was, please, God, give us more time! When Dick grew steadily worse with re-occurring bouts of pneumonia, I ran back and forth to the hospital so many times, he learned to recognize my footsteps He even made up a little song about them he titled, *Here Comes My Wife*. Both of us silently aware that time was growing shorter, he tried to comfort me as I sat by his bed. "Don't worry about me, Honey, I've made my peace with God." he said seriously. Alarmed at my tears, he joked, "If Heaven will have me!" After that, his funny side rarely came out and though I missed his marvelous sense of humor, by then, I, too, had almost forgotten how to laugh. Finally, the hospital stays turned into a long term care facility where I practically moved in with him. I brought some pictures and things to make it more like home, but truthfully, I had forgotten about Sandra's shoes. I was in for a happy surprise though when one day I told Dick that I was going to bring his favorite jacket from home. I was almost at the door when he called out to me, "Oh, Honey, bring me Sandra's shoes!" Elated that he remembered, I was overjoyed when later he held one up and said, "Wasn't it nice of Sandra to buy me these shoes?"

We made friends at the facility and Dick was very popular with them and the staff. His favorite outfit was a sweater, a black driver's cap, designer sun glasses, and of course, Sandra's shoes. The staff called him the movie director or the rock star. Dick had a wonderful personality and always wore a smile on his handsome face. When he couldn't remember his care-giver's names from day to day, it wasn't important since he'd always had a gift of being kind to strangers.

As the weeks went by, and we settled in to our new home at the care center, I gauged his progress by what he could remember. My method was tested when I had to take his beloved shoes home and wash them. In the mean time he was hospitalized with another bout of pneumonia, and it was several weeks before he returned to the care center. When he was feeling well enough to get up, I brought the shoes back, fully expecting him to be delighted to see them again. But, when I put them on him he never said a word. My heart sank. Still, I wheeled him out to the lobby, just like I always did, so he could look out the glass doors, and see our car parked out front. The sight of the big, white Lincoln usually raised his spirits, but today, he seemed not to notice it. Side by side, we sat in silence.

Suddenly, my gray skies turned blue when Dick stretched out a foot and exclaimed, "Honey, don't cha just love Sandra's shoes?"

A few weeks later Dick was rushed to the hospital again. Only this time, my beloved husband didn't return. He took my heart with him, but thanks to a special lady's ultimate gift, I have a link that keeps him close in memory . . . every time I open the closet and my eyes fall . . . on Sandra's shoes.

MY PRINCE CHARMING, DICK BELT

In Loving Memory

of

Richard G. Belt

1-11-11

A great man

Full of fun

Friend to all

Here comes my wife
My beautiful wife
I hear her footsteps
Walking my way

Here comes my wife
The love of my life
I'd know her footsteps
Ten blocks away!

THE RIGHT ANGEL

I will instruct thee and teach thee in thy ways

I will guide thee with thine eye

Ps. 32:8

SATURDAY WAS CLEANING DAY at my house, and I'd just finished the heavy work. Now, I could get to my favorite job dusting my knick-knacks I'd collected over the years. Armed with my feather-duster, I started with my latest collection of ceramic angels. Unlike my friend, Audree, who had them in every room, I had only four so far. Re-arranging the little white angels on the mirrored tray, and thinking they could use some color, I said to the Lord, please let my next angel have golden wings.

The next morning I went as usual to Dan and Audree's home to accompany them to church. After inviting me to be seated, Audree presented me with a prettily wrapped gift.

"What's the occasion?" I asked, "It isn't my birthday."

"It's a just because you're special gift. Now, please, open it!" Unwrapping my present, I gave silent thanks for this lovely couple who'd reached out to me when Dick passed away. We all became friends when Audree's mom, Violet, (whom we adored) and my husband, Dick, were hospitalized in the same care center. Now, opening the box, I was astonished to find a beautiful angel with golden wings. "I was praying for this yesterday! I exclaimed, but, how could you have known?"

"Well, the first one I chose to give you was plain white. I wrapped it and put it on the table. However, every time I walked past it, I got an unsettling feeling. Thinking perhaps it was the wrong choice, I exchanged it for the one with the golden wings. Then, I felt a peace as if God was saying "Now that's the right angel!" After church the three of us lingered over lunch until the time came I dreaded most, going home alone. Heavy silence met me when I opened the door. Walking through the quiet rooms, an intense wave of sadness swept over me. By the fireplace, I stood looking at Dick's empty chair, my heart remembering all the love and laughter we'd shared in this room where we'd spent so much of our time together. Trying not to feel abandoned, I remembered the gift my friend had given me today.

Placing the exquisite angel on the tray with the others, I felt my spirits lift as I admired the little cherub's golden wings. They seemed to hold a message from God: You're not alone, my child, I am with you always. My witty husband might have said, "See, Honey, He's still sending you angels!"

CPSIA information can be obtained at www.ICGtesting.com
Printed in the USA
BVOW030026041212

307197BV00002B/119/P